Praise for
Once Upon a Tome

✳

"Peculiarly hilarious!"—William Gibson

"An exciting new voice brimming with
self-effacing charm."—Caitlin Doughty

"Laugh-out-loud."—Garth Nix

"An enchanting billet-doux to an arcane and eccentric
world. Every page is a pleasure."—Lindsey Fitzharris

"Utterly charming."—Tom Holland

"Thank you for your extremely entertaining book,
which I have enjoyed most heartily.
The anecdotes about the bookselling profession
were as enlightening as they were amusing.
Unfortunately I have mislaid the book in question. . . .
If ever I see it again I'll try and say something
nice about it."—Neil Gaiman

✳ ✦ ✳

ONCE
UPON A
TOME

ONCE
UPON A
TOME

THE MISADVENTURES of a
RARE BOOKSELLER,
wherein the theory of the profession
is partially explained, with a variety
of insufficient examples, by

Oliver Darkshire

Interspersed with several diverting FOOTNOTES
of a comical nature, ably ILLUSTRATED by
Rohan Eason, PUBLISHED by W. W. Norton,
and humbly proposed to the consideration of the
public in this YEAR 2023

W. W. NORTON & COMPANY
Celebrating a Century of Independent Publishing

for Zero
you married a writer
so history will say you suffered
and you married a man
so history will say we were roommates

and

for my mother
who I think we can finally admit
loves me best of all her children

A Note from the Author's Supervisor

SOTHERAN'S IS VERY OLD. We have been heaving around the world since 1761, so the arrival of something as trivial as the internet was like a fly landing on the hide of a brachiosaur. One afternoon in 2012 we decided to open a Twitter account, and once in a while someone would tweet about the hilarious antics of a Guardsman in 1874, and the rest of the time we forgot about it.

No one really noticed Oliver slowly taking it over. I first became aware that he was tweeting in late 2018 when he said something like, 'Oh, I've sent this tweet, I think we might get a complaint.'

As a new managing director I thought this was something I ought to get to know about, so I accessed our Twitter account. I was instantly agog. We had gone from about four followers to a thousand. There were messages about swords and tuna and demons that apparently lived in our cellars. There were cries from the heart and jokes about owls. There was even some stuff about books.

I don't think we did receive a complaint about the tweet, but I did think I should keep an eye on things, just so I could stay in touch with the parallel universe that was being created. Oliver has spun a bizarre and extemporized multiverse out of the mundane reality of selling antiquarian books. Every now and then a broken statue of our reality emerges through the dreamscape, and sometimes Oliver engages with an urgent issue that pierces through all fantasy, but mostly he follows his whim and fancy to bring a weirdly augmented Sotheran's to the world. I usually look after the Twitter feed when Oliver is on holiday, and it is like stepping into a fever dream from which I emerge exhilarated and sweaty, as if I have completed a level of Super Mario from within the screen.

My word, it's popular though. We have getting on for forty thousand followers at the time of writing, which is phenomenal for an antiquarian bookseller, and shows not only the level of interest in the world of books but also Oliver's ability to entertain and enlighten a whole load of people we would not otherwise have reached. This book, which came about because of the Twitter feed, is a natural progression, a chance to carve a physical Rushmore from the digital mountain.

This whole crossover between the real and the virtual is, by the way, very uncomfortable for an antique bookseller. I still feel like we should be using quills. But we can't deny that the boundaries are shifting, and turning a bricks-and-mortar bookshop into a digital universe into a physical book feels very modern (but then again, so does the internal combustion engine).

So here you are, dear reader. Delve in, make discoveries, and meet some of the other Sotheranians who occupy our unique space. Not every event occurred exactly as described, and some of the characters are conflations and chimeras, and of course in my modesty I had to veto the entire twenty-page section devoted to Oliver's tribute to me as the 'most handsome, musically gifted and inspired boss in any possible universe'. But apart from that, this is all true-ish.

Chris Saunders,
Managing Director, Sotheran's

London, October 2022

Contents

Introduction: The Bookseller's Apprentice

IT WAS THE A-BOARD that gave the game away in the end. It had lost one of the stubby legs holding it upright (a victim, no doubt, of some long-forgotten street accident) and so was teetering on three. The paint had peeled off in large strips, but I could still make out most of the name: 'Henry Sotheran Ltd – Fine Books and Prints'. I had walked past twice before I'd found it, quietly tucked away on a side street known for being completely unknown. Sackville Street has a reputation for being a commercial dead-end despite being attached like a vestigial tail to Piccadilly and Regent Street, both of which bustle with umbrellas and car horns from dawn to dusk. People say businesses go to Sackville Street to die, which might explain the slightly unnerving air as I approached on that cold November morning.

I was in Sackville Street that day to interview for a job. People often ask how one gets a job at a bookshop like Sotheran's. Young and adrift in London, like many of my contemporaries I spent my days vainly grasping at shadowy career prospects which always seemed to slip through my fingers at the last minute. In a particularly dark moment, when I'd drifted into some far corner of the internet on my search, I saw an advertisement for a bookshop seeking an apprentice. It wasn't a particularly good advertisement. The pay was Victorian, the expected duties nebulous, and the whole thing had an air of desperation about it. More comfortingly, however, no prior experience was necessary, and within a day I'd received a call asking me to attend an interview with the manager.

On the day of the interview, I was early – in the days before I became involved in books I frequently was. Striding confidently at the double door, I gave it a hearty push, the kind of push someone might make who you would hire on the spot. It didn't move, instead rattling about noisily. I yanked it. By this point I could see shadowy figures inside staring icily at my abortive entry attempts, but I persevered. Pushing the right-hand door, I stumbled inside, mumbling a half-hearted apology which was swallowed up by the diorama stretching out before me.

It's the smell that hits you first. Vellichor. There's something wistful about old books when they are gathered in one place. They have a faintly unsatisfied smell, as if they're all distantly aware that they've missed their chance to be a worldwide smash hit. I looked around at the colourful shelves of books, tables piled high with suspicious articles, crooked furniture and misplaced literary paraphernalia. You don't think of the word 'colourful' when you envision an old bookshop, but it's true of all the ones I know. The pillars holding the creaking roof aloft blocked out a full view of the shop floor, which only appeared accessible in its furthest reaches by dodging between dangerously stacked piles of classic literature. People milled about in the shadows, doors creaking open and closed. The only sounds were the curmudgeonly groaning of cases, the shuffling of feet, and a phone bleeping unanswered somewhere in the dark.

I'm not sure quite how long I stood there taking it all in. Eventually, I was saved from myself by a gregarious man with a mop of silver hair and a bad back who it transpired was Andrew, the manager. To this day I've never met anyone with quite such a talent for defusing an uncomfortable situation. I've seen people walk in ready to burn the shop to the ground, and three minutes with Andrew had them agreeing to dinner at some later point, buying a book and leaving with a baffled expression as if they couldn't quite remember why they came into the shop in the first place. Sotheran's is a small place, as I would come to find out, and if I'd thought the manager would be a far-off and unapproachable figure I was quickly disabused of that notion.

I was led down the grand stairs in the middle of the shop to the lower floor, and through the Print Gallery filled with posters, illustrations and other maddeningly distracting wonders. We breezed past them into a side room crammed with bibliographic reference books. Andrew gave me a rather apologetic look as he tried, with limited success, to extract two chairs from the debris. The door closed, and everything fell silent. Cramped bookshelves muffle noise from outside, a strange effect which also helps insulate the shop from the traffic on surrounding roads. If you're used to working or living in any large city, and especially one like London, you know that the background hum of cars and engines seeps into your soul – there are very few places where you can escape from the constant muttering of the streets. But bookshops are one of them.

Perched on chairs in the tiny room, there was barely space for both of us to sit, and Andrew seemed to realize this as he inched a little further back into a stack of old bookselling magazines. This, he explained, was the Catalogue Room. Its purpose, he confessed, roughly translated to 'this is where we put things when there is nowhere else for them to go'. Several months into my fruitless London job search, this felt oddly apt.

Part of Andrew's knack for putting people at ease was his eagle eye for reading people from a distance. It's a prerequisite for any decent bookseller really, but Andrew was, and remains, the expert. After no more than ten seconds sizing me up, he spent the rest of the interview idly chatting about the problems the shop had faced finding reliable new staff in recent years. It transpired – or so he confessed as I sat transfixed by this unexpected frankness – that each year the shop had hired some bright young thing, a star on the rise with degrees and qualifications to match, thinking themselves to have secured the Perfect Bookseller. Alas, in every case the prodigy lasted about six months before buggering off into the stratosphere of the art world where wages (and proximity to daylight) were in greater abundance. Andrew was looking for something different this time. He was looking for someone who wanted to stay, who was in it for the long haul. The staff, he explained, were getting whiplash from learning one new name a year and it was all very inconvenient. He laid out the terms: the hired apprentice would stay on for at least two years under a training scheme to transform them into a competent anti-quarian bookseller, at which point the company hoped they would become a full-time member of staff.

I'll admit to you, reader, that I nodded like a performing seal. It's true that the wages for an apprentice bookseller seemed to have been frozen around when the Old Curiosity Shop opened for business in 1840, but it was better than the little to which I had become accustomed. More than that, compared to my recurring nightmare of cowering misera-bly in a cubicle, the job seemed like a lifeline. Even if I couldn't move without threatening to dislodge some precar-iously situated and priceless relic of company history.

The interview was over almost as soon as it began. I remember thinking I must have botched the whole thing terribly, because we were in and out before I really had time to process what was happening. I was sent home with a cheery smile and a 'we'll be in touch in a few days'. My heart sank.

At three o'clock that afternoon I received a call offering me the job. I will never be sure why. I have a small suspicion that they threw darts at a wheel of fortune, or simply got me confused with someone else and never found a good moment to correct the mistake. Regardless, a few days later I was walking back up to the double doors in a rather bat-tered old suit and with a new sense of purpose.

It's funny, thinking back, that my journey started as simply as this. A half-hearted advertisement stumbled across online. A furtive interview. A quick polish of the shoes (never repeated). And suddenly I was a rare bookseller.

Antiquarian gourd of nebulous origin, confidently engraved with the likeness of Queen Victoria. Desirable.

ANTIQUARIAN
& GENERAL

A primer on the art of bookselling, general occurrences,
confessions and misapprehensions of the literary kind &c.

IT IS AMAZING how high a proportion of our stock is not actually books. Tradition has it that the literature is lumped in with miscellaneous nonsense and general bric-a-brac on the shelves at Sotheran's under a department called Antiquarian and General – a polite way of saying that no one really knows what else to do with it. As an apprentice with no skills (and later in my career as a bookseller with no skills) I was expected to help out with this sprawling department, which encompasses much of the strangeness Sotheran's has to offer. You never know quite what you'll find in Antiquarian and General. Fortunately for me, it also contains everything which the average person might be looking for. You want an Austen? Wonderful. It's probably over there near the bust of Prince Albert, in the cabinet above some rather ugly Byron we've never been able to shift. In one corner, roosting on a rickety stool and clutching a tankard of tea, is James.

1

James

IF I THOUGHT MY INTERVIEW at the shop had given me an idea of what to expect from my colleagues, I was mistaken. Until I turned up at the shop for my first day of work, the manager Andrew was the only colleague I'd met. His calm, sanguine attitude was innately soothing. He remains in my mind the archetype of what it means to work in antiquarian books, inhabiting an effortless serenity in the face of chaos that I have always struggled to emulate. This sublime state of being, I feel, was perhaps cultivated by keeping potential sources of stress (such as a bumbling apprentice) at arm's length. And so it transpired that I was passed on to James for training.

If Andrew was the heart that quietly, patiently kept blood pumping around the shop, then James was the spine that kept it upright. Tall and slightly crooked, he had the air of a scarecrow that had been left out in the sun for too long. From his paper-strewn desk in a dimly lit corner of the shop he watched over the books, guarding them with a suspender-clad perspicacity cultivated over many years to drive away shoplifters, ne'er-do-wells and birds of ill omen. I spent much of my first year under James's tutelage, and in many ways he encapsulated something of an older time; it might seem impertinent to describe him as a fossil, but his endless, loving repairs on the shop left an imprint on the place, and I suppose eventually it shaped him in return.* Loping around like a grizzled but bookish wolf, he handled all the day-to-day mundane affairs of the shop. Thus my apprenticeship fell into his hands in the same way as anything else no one really wanted to deal with. It came to my attention several years into my role that no one in the shop apart from James knew where the rubbish went, who took it anywhere, or what happened to it. As far as anyone was concerned, it just vanished. (It transpired that James didn't *want* anyone to know, for reasons which will become apparent.)

Supposedly James had been apprenticed as a boat builder (*not* at a dockyard – the distinction was oddly important to him) before he wandered into Henry Sotheran Ltd one day and never left. Either way, everything he knew (and he knew *everything*) was the result of being at the bookshop from mid-morning till dusk each day for decades. In hindsight I am very grateful that I had him looking out for me during those first few months, but I didn't really have time for feelings of gratitude as they placed me at a Munchkin-sized desk in front of the double doors. It was explained to me that the desk had been designed for Victorian ladies,

---

* I use the word 'repairs' generously, because his well-meaning efforts rarely resulted in the offending door, shelf or case functioning in the same way after he had finished fixing it. James was a handyman of the self-taught variety, and the rest of the staff took the rather sensible position that it is rarely a good idea to argue overlong with a man who uses a hammer to solve most of his problems.

not for the lumbering six feet of clumsiness which now sat behind it, meaning I essentially had to ride the wretched thing side-saddle for years. I have, for various reasons, spent most of my bookselling career behind desks that are far too small for me, but this very first desk I resented most of all.

A few days passed peaceably in the shop, sat at my tiny desk, before I realized I hadn't really done anything. I was used to a busy environment – my previous job was doing paperwork at a legal firm. I was dreadfully bad at that, and fled the situation before they could fire me. But the change of pace was jarring. At Sotheran's, much to my amazement, the phone didn't really ring at all (sometimes for hours). People sat quietly at their desks, working on something peculiar and arcane which I couldn't pretend to understand. Sometimes people wandered in, and James would swoop down from the rafters to direct them to the right shelves. Andrew, the manager, sat at the desk adjacent to me, occasionally kindly asking if I was doing all right. Yes, I was doing all right, I would confirm, too scared to mention that I wasn't sure what I was supposed to be doing. Eventually it dawned on me that if I didn't ask for something to do, my ossified remains might eventually be found cradling the tiny desk in my arms by a team of confused archaeologists. No sooner, however, had the thought entered my mind than James manifested from a shadowy enclave with a box of books. I was to be taught cataloguing.

At the time I was baffled by the events unfolding before me, having no idea at all what was meant by cataloguing, even if I was glad to have something to do. The task seemed to involve describing the books using odd words, and it was a much better pastime than sitting there twiddling my thumbs.* The books I was being asked to handle were not rare books, but things James had picked up on his many attempts to sneak second-hand books into the shop. As a new recruit in a shop full of mysterious colleagues whose workings I didn't really understand, this was perfect teaching material – stuff I could afford to get vastly wrong without any real consequence. It spoke to a schism among staff, however, about what it means to be an antiquarian bookseller.

Though they might all seem the same at a glance, second-hand books are not always rare books, and rare books are not always antiquarian books. James was a bookseller who, despite his expertise in all things book-related, wanted to sell second-hand books. He enjoyed selling £10 copies of anything he could find in a car boot sale or a cellar, or retrieve from the bin of a publisher's remainder stock, to anyone who walked in off the street. He had no interest in computers, no interest in cataloguing rare books, and he marked up everything in a manner that wasn't technically criminal but probably should have been. It was a bookselling model that harked back to days gone by when people would (I hear) walk in off the street and depart with piles of books loaded on to their carriage. James was very fond of waxing lyrical about the days when people were less picky – he considered the 'modern' and technological

---

* For an explanation of this dark art, see 5. Cataloguing for Beginners.

avenues of bookselling to be an extravagant conceit. If he had to sit on a stack of books for ten years before they sold, then so be it – a book will find its proper owner in due course. The true spirit of book buying, as far as he was concerned, did not debase itself with trivialities like 'What will I eat later?' or 'How will I pay my rent?'.

Unlike many of the other staff, who preferred to deal in rare items worth larger sums of money, delivering them safely into the hands of enthusiastic collectors and prestigious institutions, James just wanted to sell books. Any books. And so each day he would arrive on his creaking bicycle, trussed up with another bulging crate of second-hand whodunnits or 1990s train guides, and lug them inside. My apprenticeship served as something of a laundering scheme for these books. James would pass them to me to teach me about them, and then spirit them away into the back of the shop before Andrew could say 'where are you taking all those hideous books, get back here this instant'.

2

Browsers and Dilettantes

I THINK IT'S IMPORTANT to pause for a moment and explain that antiquarian booksellers have a complex relationship with their customers. I came into bookselling completely unprepared, which is perhaps a mercy because I might otherwise have fled in the opposite direction without ever looking back. I am rather generously using the word 'customer' here, in the absence of a better term, to describe anyone who darkens our threshold. In truth only a fraction of the people who enter an antiquarian bookshop have any intention of purchasing a book.

Now, I'm not a gregarious person by nature. I was the kind of toddler who was told they needed to play more with the other children, and the kind of teenager who spent their time being told that if they didn't have anything nice to say to other people then they should leave them alone.* There are very few job positions open for a twenty-year-old with a bad attitude and no higher education, and unfortunately almost all of these involve dealing with the general public in one manner or another. Looking back, I think part of what attracted me to the world of rare books was the fanciful, naive idea that it might involve fewer uncomfortable encounters with strangers than a supermarket kiosk, or vagrancy.

When you're watching the shop floor of an antiquarian bookshop, there's usually a fairly steady trickle of people gingerly entering from the street throughout the day. Young. Old. Bespectacled. Tattooed. The vast majority are going to wander around looking haunted or asking questions, and a small number are going to buy books. Sadly, it really is

---

* My mother has never let me forget the occasion on which a four-year-old Oliver, on being told he needed to stop sitting by himself, took the opportunity to stand up and show his arse to the poor teacher in question. Alas the punishment, being sent to the reading corner, was not altogether discouraging.

impossible to tell one from the other at a glance, so everyone has to be treated as if they might suddenly whip out a gigantic bag of gold bars and purchase the place. Equally possible is that some disreputable-looking wanderer might surprise you with a Gutenberg Bible. There's really no way of knowing what's about to happen in any given moment.

When I took up my place behind the front desk at Sotheran's, the expectation was that any request from a customer should be politely entertained where possible.* It was one of the stipulations laid out in the Sotheran's Staff Manual, and James insisted on it. You would often find him poring over a vintage *A–Z* of London, pointing someone towards an establishment that no longer existed, or unwittingly directing them into a construction zone filled with territorial rats. He would give out umbrellas from our umbrella stand, only remembering as the customer disappeared into the rain that the only reason the device in question hadn't been stolen already was that it had a large hole in it. He was a total gentleman, and a public menace.

It's probably the cosiness of a bookshop that leads people to treat it more like a second home, or a hotel, than a place of business. There's a certain kind of person we see all the time who strides in looking for something which is definitely not a book. Staplers. Printers. Spoons. They'll trumpet over the threshold armed with a toothy smile, with

---

* Fortunately for us, most of the mundane requests we have to consider are of a harmless but time-consuming nature. I consider it a mercy that no one had the audacity to ask James for the keys to the safe.

a view to finding some generous polymath who can direct them to what they need. It's possible that in other book-shops they do find this kind of help, which would explain the alarming regularity with which people wander in asking for things we clearly don't sell. I've printed out solid reams of directions, taught elderly women how Google Maps works ('Oh, so the picture *moves*, does it? Do another one, I want to see my house'), stood in the street desperately miming the phrase 'turn around and go back the way you came' to a gentleman old enough to have witnessed the fall of Carthage – all in a day's work for the common-or-garden book dealer. Our imagined status as mysterious guardians of all knowledge leads people to treat booksellers as terrestrial genies, spiriting up the answer to any problem from the bottom of our fusty old pockets.

A bone of contention for quite some time in the Sotheran's firmament was the dreaded question, traditionally uttered with an apologetic grimace, 'Can I Use Your Bathroom?' An innocent request, you might think. Sotheran's has always been blessed with spacious, well-appointed lavatories buried at the back of the shop near the cellars. The casual London shopper is somehow able to sense this from a mile away, and we frequently receive visitors looking to answer the call of nature in an antiquarian retail environment. It took the Incident of 2014 for the bathrooms to be sealed off from public use, the particulars of which are not for the faint of heart, and I shall spare you the grisly details.

3

Collectors

G IVEN THE GENERAL IRRITATION that most casual customers pose, you might wonder why booksellers ever
open their doors at all. The reason is Collectors. Like an
ugly duckling morphing into a golden goose, sometimes a
casual browser will evolve into a book collector. It's impossible
to say what catalyses this change. Some primal magpie-
adjacent urge begins to burn under the surface, and one
dark day they make a simple choice whence there is no
return . . . they purchase an old book. It might seem innocuous, but this is the first in thirty-nine ineluctable steps towards
being a ninety-year-old hermit in a house full of books,
complaining that your ungrateful children do not appreciate your Library. Long sleepless nights as a bookseller are
spent trying to figure out what causes the transformation
from one state to another, but the mystery as yet remains
unsolved. Be that as it may, collectors provide the vast
majority of bookshop revenue, because they are absolutely
insatiable.

Under the banner of 'book collector' you'll find a host
of strange and wonderful people, united by their obsession
with acquiring and sitting on a hoard of papery treasures.
Some of them make a point of coming in regularly, some
communicate by mail only, and some like to send delegates
from overseas carrying a list of cryptic instructions to be
carried out over a six-day period. They will often have very
specific interests and needs, and if you want to retain their

custom then you'll need to remember what they are, what books are in their collection already, and a host of other details. Then, when they appear, you manifest relevant items out of thin air with a flourish, a behaviour which appears to the onlooker to derive from extra-sensory perception but actually originates in decades of careful, hypervigilant note-taking.

There are two kinds of collector you really have to watch out for. Untrained observers think there are more, but there's really only two.

Smaugs, like their namesake, like to amass vast lairs full of precious items. They are sometimes wealthy, but most are comfortably situated enough to spread their collecting habits over many areas. The main quality they share is that of the polymath: one subject area is not enough, when they could have fifty. They may not know exactly what is in their collection, but they'd rather buy three copies than risk missing out. As you can imagine, this makes booksellers very happy to see them, because you can be sure that no matter what strange book you have waiting on the shelves, a Smaug will appreciate it. They will never snub you for suggesting a book on garderobes. When they finally pass on or dispense with their library, their dragon hoard is released back into the bookselling world in a great flood, inciting a minor gold rush for the most precious objects.

Draculas have one very specific interest that sustains them, and their collecting habits are centred around it. Rare plants. Gothic table decorations. Calligraphy. They'll procure and sequester anything in that line of scholarship, and your chances of selling them a book are directly proportional to how close you can make it look to their field of interest. You have to invite them over the threshold with tempting acquisitions, but a relationship can be quite rewarding, as you'll rarely find anyone quite as devoted to their area of specialism. Furthermore, if you need to pick someone's brains, they are usually very happy to share their knowledge. Some will even lend you books, or invite you over to look at a new find. Some of our closest relationships with clients are with this kind of specialized collector, cultivated over decades.

Every book collector comes under one of those two banners, and the smart bookseller learns to identify them as quickly as possible. If you keep offering a Dracula books outside their current fixation, they will vanish into the night and find another bookseller who better understands their tastes, and if you offer a Smaug only a limited, curated selection of content, they'll quickly get bored (or, worse, stop spending money). Managing the expectations and desires of collectors is the heart of the rare book business, a strange kind of symbiosis in which the least social of people, each allergic to daylight in our own way, come together to serve a mutually beneficial purpose.

The reliance of old bookshops on collectors to keep them afloat has a downside. It's the richer clientele who are fond of delivering the kind of really involved requests that haunt us in the night hours. Keeping their custom (and not losing them to a rival bookshop) means making their priorities your priorities. If a visiting billionaire hands you a ceremonial art object covered in metal knives and asks you to send it to his home on a small island south of New

Zealand, then it gets sent. Never mind that the postal service doesn't like accepting knives, that you can't put 'stabbing relic' on a customs form without being blacklisted as a terrorist organization, or that no one can lift the wretched thing.

4

Book Runners

IRRITATINGLY, WHEN YOU SELL A BOOK, it immediately needs replacing with something else. Unlike at a new bookshop, however, one can't simply go online and order ten more rare books from the aether to plug a gap – not least because the margins on buying books from other dealers are very slim indeed. No, the really valuable stock is free range – coming from outside the trade, where the bookseller can make a decent profit on it. To this end, like Scheherazade running amok with a company credit card, booksellers employ a thousand and one different methods of acquiring books. We'll come to others later, but perhaps the most peculiar of all the book sources we ritually engage is the Book Runner.

A tradition which seems to come from a time beyond living memory, a book runner is a savvy individual who finds cheap books overlooked in distant parishes or second-hand shops, and then takes them into a city where the competition is fierce, making a tidy sum for themselves in the process. The city bookseller, who has a client list and the impact of a bricks-and-mortar location to leverage, then lists the book at a sensible price, and everyone walks away happy.

There's no society of book runners. I don't believe there's anyone who teaches them or instructs them, but they pop up around old bookshops quite reliably without any prompting whatsoever. It almost seems a rule of nature.

It's not an easy (or popular) job, that of a book runner, so between bookshops there's a certain amount of silent competition for their favour – you want them bringing you the good stuff, after all. There's a danger that, if you buy nothing at all on one occasion, they might visit one of your competitors first the next time. On the other hand, if you buy too many things you don't really want from them, you're likely to be staring at that mistake sitting on your shelf year on year until you either retire or die. Which brings us to Mrs Hawthorne.

Mrs Hawthorne's husband died some time ago, leaving behind an impressive library of gardening books on their estate, which the shop bought from her over several years. Eventually, as the stock of gardening books ran dry, she covertly began to insert newly purchased books as if they were part of the original collection, presumably having become accustomed to the income. As time passed, it began to dawn on us that the books were not from the original library, and that Mrs Hawthorne had evolved (like a shawl-draped Pokémon) into a book runner. Which would have been fine if her personal taste in books had been anything other than demented.

Mrs Hawthorne was never one to be deterred, and rarely one for taking advice. So our gentle insinuations that she might want to guide her selection of wares towards something saleable were not something she was prepared to countenance. Neither, in fact, did she register the explicit lists of titles we were looking for, or the veiled threats of a restraining order if she didn't stop lugging in sacks of books. It's unclear to this day how she even managed it, showing a wiry (and frankly unholy) strength that quite belied her diminutive, ancient frame. Time went on, and as weeks turned into months, the drones in the Sotheran's hive mind clearly reached the only sane conclusion that avoided bloodshed: the shop would be buying books from Mrs Hawthorne for ever, and those books would be placed in the dark somewhere, written off as a necessary expense in the name of keeping the peace.

A healthy bookshop engages a range of book runners similar to Mrs Hawthorne, all of whom no doubt have some clandestine reason for choosing a life hauling sacks of books from place to place rather than settling down somewhere. It has always confused me that no one seems to know they exist, because without them the London book trade would come to a juddering halt.

5

Cataloguing for Beginners

EXTRA-ILLUSTRATED, MY FRIEND, that's what you want to call it.' James is picking through a set of books he's left with me for cataloguing. He picks one up and flicks through the pages. 'A tad faded . . . no, not faded . . . mellowed. A little mellowed on the spine.' I'm busy making notes so he keeps going. 'Attractively so, I'd wager.' He looks over my shoulder at what I've written so far. 'No, see, you can't say all the books are different colours, that won't sell them. How about . . .' He mulls it over. 'Perhaps a "harlequin set"?' He winks. 'Scarce thus.'

He heads back to his desk, pleased with a job well done. 'Now you see, young Oliver, that's, uh . . . what do they call it, Georg? Entrepreneurial spirit?'

There is a muffled grumble from behind a shelf: 'They call it bullshit, James.'

Running the Travel and Exploration department, a blighted role which before his arrival had chewed up and spat out three or four booksellers in short order, Georg has proven utterly immovable by the unholy forces which drove out his predecessors. He can often be found wandering outside the shop, smoking and drinking coffee on the kerb of Sackville Street in his favourite leather waistcoat.

If you've ever seen one of those nature documentaries where the tiny birds eat flies off a larger animal, then you'll already have a good grasp of my symbiotic relationship with Georg. He can destroy a computer simply by proximity, which means I spend a fair chunk of time at his desk figuring out the precise way in which it has melted down this time. In return for my ambiguously proficient computer expertise, Georg provides wisdom and advice, which for a beleaguered apprentice sounded like a rather wonderful arrangement.

As part of his role running the Travel and Exploration department, Georg trades in books on just about every place on the globe.* I highly suspect he has read all of them, too, because his vast well of peculiar stories never seems to run dry. He tells them in such a spellbinding manner that you always believe them, though I suppose that when it comes to memoirs and histories the truth must be a relative thing. Travelogues, diaries, entertainingly incorrect antique maps . . . he knows them all. In the truest sense of the word, he's a savant.

Learning how to catalogue properly is an essential part of bookselling, though exactly what constitutes 'properly' will change depending on who you ask. As an apprentice bookseller, it was learning the intricacies of the cataloguing process from my colleagues which consumed any spare time I had when not hauling boxes or fixing Georg's desktop.

In days gone by, when dinosaurs and Mrs Hawthornes ruled the earth, booksellers didn't have the advantage of colour photography, or the luxury of printing out reams of

---

* He insists he is not a collector, just that he buys books and keeps some at home.

pictures to send to book collectors. The majority of selling was performed (and to a certain extent still is) using gigantic sales brochures crammed with information on the newest books in stock, printed in tiny type and shipped off to the homes of book collectors around the country, who would eagerly flip through them, scanning the rows and rows of text for juicy treasures. Collectors being as fastidious as they are, booksellers were faced with a unique challenge – to describe as accurately as possible a specimen of a particular book, communicating all the flaws and merits of that very specific copy, while using as little ink and space as possible. Thus the art of cataloguing, which invokes an entire dialect of terms, abbreviations and insinuations to paint a picture of a book without leaning too heavily on images. On any given day, it's very likely this is what the booksellers are doing, lurking with their heads in a pile of books, brows furrowed as they try to work out if their copy is *supposed* to have nineteen pictures.

The actual day-to-day minutiae of cataloguing encompasses a vast array of tasks that take a book from 'I bought this' to 'This is now on the shelves'. It involves identifying the edition, checking for damage, writing some advertising copy and logging this all into the archaic computer system so it can be referenced later. The hardest part, though, lies in recording precisely in what ways a book has survived the ravages of time. An entire lexicon of book-related terminology has evolved over hundreds of years for exactly this purpose – terminology that means absolutely nothing to the average observer. It's traditional to adopt this baroque language when describing your books, for two reasons. The first is that the specific language of the book trade allows you to be exceedingly accurate and precise without using hundreds of words, and the second is that the elegance of it serves to dull the blow a little. Most rare books come with some minor defects, but that doesn't mean one has to be rude about it. It's much more charming to describe a book as 'foxed' than to tell someone that the pages have developed an unsightly mottling, and that if this were a zombie movie we'd already have taken it out back and put it out of its misery. It's convention to call a sheepskin binding 'roan', and parchment made from calfskin is oft baptized 'vellum'. If we call a book 'sophisticated', we're saying that we know the book was tampered with, faked or 'someone tried very hard to make this *look* like a first edition', but that we also feel this perhaps *adds* to its historical value rather than subtracts. It's a feature, we argue, not a bug. Using the correct terminology is part of a performance, an elaborate ritual, a secret handshake performed on the part of the bookseller to entice discerning clients.

As I learned how the trade worked, James would bring over piles of books to my desk, and armed with a copy of Carter's *ABC for Book Collectors** I would set to work trying to identify each item one after another. Not expensive books, not for an apprentice – anything with a spine and pages would do. Whenever I looked confused, someone would wander over and holler at me a term I didn't understand,

---

* A tome notable not only for being a helpful primer on rare book terminology, but also because the writer was an incorrigible crab apple who hated just about everyone, and made that very clear.

which I would dutifully note down time after time until the associations began to stick. It took a while to get to grips with the basics, because there is so much to learn before you can even engage with the fundamentals. Is it a red book? Well, you can't say that. It's actually maroon. Or burgundy. And the binding? Leather. But what kind? No, that's not cow, it's roan. It's not speckled, it's lightly becankered. It's not half morocco, it's *quarter* morocco, which has nothing to do with the country and something to do with goats.

Further to all this confusion, your average antiquarian bookseller is expected to make some comment as to the condition of the book. You might, for example, think to say 'this book is in *fine* condition' or perhaps 'this book is in *good* condition'. Both would seem quite reasonable ways to describe a book without any obvious flaws, one might think, but in this context they are two different things. You may only describe a book as Fine if it has recently nestled in the bosom of an angel, and a Good book might as well be on fire, because you've inadvertently just called it a dog's breakfast. Heaven forbid you ever designate anything a Reading Copy. I attempted this once (and only once) before James descended upon me clutching a copy of my description in white knuckles, and in a quiet voice made it very clear that I would on no account use those words again in that order.

Much like any other discipline, you never really stop learning how to catalogue, because it's a process that evolves with your understanding of the material. Unlike other disciplines, book cataloguing is less an art, not really a science, and more of a completely unstandardized, decentralized carnival fire. What I haven't told you yet is that 90 per cent of booksellers will have their own professional interpretation of what each word means in a given context.

Imagine the scene. There I am, puzzling over a book bigger than my armspan which rests in the cradle of my desk like a bible on a lectern, idly looking way out of my depth. James drifts by. Well, that's a Folio, he says, on account of the size. It's a big one, no more to it than that. No sooner have I picked up a pen than Georg drifts by. Not a Folio, he advises, looking at my notes. You see, if you look at the way the pages are arranged, you'll see it's actually a Quarto. He wanders off to attend to something else, before someone else chances past. Technically an Imperial Octavo, they say, getting out a ruler as if drawing a dagger. Battle is joined, and a merry period is spent with various parties firing pointed salvos across the work floor, as the book remains completely uncatalogued. The disagreement is fundamentally unresolvable, because no one is technically wrong, and the row continues until everyone gets tired and the book is discarded into a pile of problematic tomes to be dealt with at a later date. It's all just a matter of carefully crafted opinion, and eventually the individual bookseller has to make a call and live with it.

Most bookshops inhabited by more than a single bookseller will have what is called a House Style, which all the booksellers internally adhere to. These styles are more or less constrictive depending on the bookseller, and Sotheran's allows its sellers a fair amount of freedom to interpret. Weep for Oliver, then, because as time went by (and more people got involved) the determination of each bookseller to make sure I received a proper education was matched only by their zeal in making sure it was their language I adhered to. To this day I will still find people suggesting a full stop here, or a comma there, or staging a group intervention in response to a rogue apostrophe.

6

Customer Service

ABOUT A WEEK after I first clambered astride my tiny desk, a faint light came on at the back of Andrew's skull and slowly meandered into the frontal lobe over the course of several hours.* I should have a contract, it was suggested. Hadn't that been sorted out already? No? Oh dear. A call was placed using one of the unpredictable desk phones to another workstation down in the basement level, and the General Secretary was summoned.

It's not that Evelyn had an outwardly terrifying appearance, because she didn't. Friendly faced and softly spoken, she was the very model of your favourite aunt – and yet she carried herself in such a way as if to suggest your resistance

---

* Andrew's strategy of mulling over a task was an excellent administrative strategy for cutting down on wasteful busy work, the general philosophy being that if a task didn't need two or maybe three reminders to make it happen, then it wasn't important enough to bother with in the first place.

was futile. Imagine, if you will, that after crossing the Alps Hannibal decided to retire (sans elephants) to a small book-shop and take up clerical work as a hobby. You'd have every reason to believe that he wasn't going to eviscerate you and decorate the halls with your intestines, but you'd also know that it wasn't fully outside the realms of possibility. Her name was (and still is) spoken with a certain tone of rever-ence in the halls of Sotheran's. Evelyn, it seemed, was to handle the *particulars*, and handle them she did.

Even when you're running a rare bookshop as old as Sotheran's, one must eventually get down to the gritty busi-ness of money. Fortunately, the booksellers are not expected to deal directly with the repercussions of their actions, as all the tricksome financial details are handled by the mysteri-ous Accounts department, kept at arm's length from customers and suppliers alike. There is a lock on the door of the accounts office to keep anyone from wandering in (including booksellers) unless they can remember the access code. By tradition the Sotheran's accounting team operates in a pair, like slippers or beavers, keeping a low profile to avoid the predations of people looking to have their invoices paid.

Reluctant to adopt a new technology in anything but the direst of circumstances, the financial operations at Sotheran's are managed in part using a gigantic ledger too large to be easily shifted from the desk, in a convenient shorthand illegible to anyone but the person who inscribed it. Banks of filing cabinets and boxes of papers are piled on top of each other, arranged according to some bespoke turn of logic coined decades ago, and from which financial records are spirited forth to contest ancient disputes. In short, it's where the money comes from, and where the money goes. The rest is a mystery to anyone but the accountants, who are not telling.

Further to this, Evelyn handled any paperwork which arrived at the shop and didn't hold any interest for the booksellers. All of the paperwork, in truth. Her job amounted to General Secretary, though I don't think we will ever quite know the half of everything she quietly took care of behind the scenes. Her little office tucked away under the stairs contained files and files of neatly organized papers stretching back for decades, each kept for a very specific purpose that slowly faded from her memory over time until they became part of her office. The day on which I was to receive my contract called for one of these papers to be retrieved, which seemed to delight her as she delved into the mass of identical-looking files, paper flying every-where. Entire sheaves of forms and confidential information began to stack up in intimidating piles, slowly obscuring her from view as a dark sea of dusty binders parted before her. I did not offer help – it would have been a superficial gesture at best, and I knew better than to interrupt genius at work. Eventually she popped back out of the melee clutching a blank contract and a typewritten copy of the Sotheran's Staff Manual 'recently' updated by James in the early 1990s, which dictated the rituals by which the book-seller should engage with the customers.

The Sotheran's Staff Manual remained in my desk for over a year before I actually found time to read it. As far as I know only a single copy exists. It contains all of James's tried and tested advice for staying on top of a rare bookshop.

Never be intimidated by customers who say that they always get a discount.

Truly his most valuable advice, because around half of all Sotheran's customers will try and convince you that they are owed money off their order. They know the owner, they'll say. They donated a kidney. They have a blood pact with the directors. A bookseller must stand firm in the face of this and laugh away any request as if the person who made it was joking (invariably they are not).

Be on your guard with groups of people, even pairs. While one person causes a rumpus, the other may be helping himself.

An honourable mention for correct use of the word 'rumpus'. James was in the habit of following groups of people around the shop, fluttering after them like a bird of prey ready to swoop down with talons extended. To my mind, this was the reason they kept acting strangely, but James was convinced everyone was in cahoots to loot the place until an exchange of hard cash proved otherwise.

Thieves may try to wear you down by staying in the shop so long that you stop watching them. Never reduce your vigilance.

Paranoid he may have been, but he had a point. It's not unusual for people to linger in the shop for hours at a time, and it's hard to remember to keep an eye on them for all that time. After the ten-minute mark I usually find my concentration slipping.

Do not talk to a customer from a sitting position, particularly if the customer is a woman.

I reject this in its entirety.

Never talk to a customer with your hands in your trouser pockets.

This seems overly optimistic to me, in that it assumes my pockets are not already full of measuring tapes, leaking pens and gigantic rings of keys.

A customer hurried is easily lost but so is a customer given too long to make up their mind. Persuasion should be gentle and careful; and above all, finely timed.

For all his dubious advice concerning sitting and pockets, this was the area where he displayed true mastery. James knew exactly how long to leave a customer with a book before he returned to prod them in the right direction towards buying it. He understood, in a deeper way than everyone around him, that a rare book is a luxury that no one really needs in the same way they need food, or housing. It is a decadence, one that James was adept at convincing you was absolutely essential for your future happiness. He would do this by determining (from years of practice) exactly how long he needed to spend locating a book for you that would lead you to feel a sense of commitment towards it. He already spent half an hour finding it for you, after all, and wouldn't that time be wasted if you didn't take it?* He'd then make sure he left you in a quiet space to inspect it (it's the least you can do) and disappear for a while, because no polite person would leave before at least making their excuses to the salesperson who'd gone so far out of their way to help.

Most customers automatically reject the first thing shown to them where there are a number of desirable alternatives. Doubt is often expressed about the second choice proffered . . .

When he did finally reappear, it would be with another book. One related to the first, which he knew wasn't quite right. The customer would by this point be ready to hand the first book back and make their excuses, but the appearance of a second option ensnared them in a net of mutual obligation. The poor customer would remain in place for another turning of the clock while they pretended to give this second book the same level of scrutiny they'd given the first. Fair is fair, after all.

. . . and the third becomes easily acceptable (the customer has determined that they are using their power of choice). The book you really want to sell should be brought out third . . .

---

* I have since learned that this is called the Sunk Cost Fallacy, and James leveraged it with terrifying precision.

James would return for a third time when the customer's impatience had reached a low simmer, having resolved to reject both the first and second books for whatever reason sprang to mind. Before they could sputter out more than a few words, James would go for the jugular, producing a third book which was vastly superior to the two he had already offered. This time he wouldn't vanish, taking a moment to comment on exactly why it was special, and how rare an opportunity it was. He'd hover there, ready to take payment. More often than not the customer would buckle under the pressure, and agree to take the book, sporting the kind of suspicious and wide-eyed look someone might adopt if they were mugged by a grizzly bear in a party hat. The most peculiar thing is that after a certain number of weeks had passed, the customer would convince themselves, as James correctly predicted, that the entire experience had been voluntary and fuelled by their own good discrimination. This would prompt them to show up to the shop a second time, where the process would begin again until the customer was entirely in the grip of a specialized variant of Stockholm syndrome.

. . . this does not mean resort to hoover-type salesmanship.

7

Cryptids

IT WAS A BITTERLY COLD AFTERNOON when I met my first bookshop cryptid, and I remember it well. At first, I mistook her for a Dracula, haunting the shelves near the back with something approaching intent. It was a matter of the way she walked which made my hackles rise. Long skirts hid her feet, and she gave the impression of gliding from place to place without touching the floor. In a low voice which I recall with unnerving clarity, she asked me whether I had met her before. No, I said, as politely as I could, I didn't think I had. She smiled, showing too many teeth for comfort, and then asked if I would like to hear her sing. She had a beautiful singing voice, she insisted.

The criteria for identifying a cryptid, as opposed to any of the people who come into the bookshop for legitimate non-scary reasons, are threefold:

1. They have never purchased a book, a quality that neither time nor association will alter.
2. They are peculiar enough that you have doubts they are real; *or,* you have never seen them but have frequently witnessed evidence of their passage.
3. They repeatedly return to the scene of the crime as if drawn by a lure.

A bookshop as old as Sotheran's is blessed with a number of common-or-garden cryptid varieties, most of which have the decency to darken our doorstep only once in a blue moon.

The Spindleman is a mysterious visitant with hair like straw and the temper of Rumpelstiltskin. He turns up more frequently than I would like, lugging an entire cartful of books, which he attempts to sell to anyone who will countenance the idea. Alas, one must treat the Spindleman with the same caution you would treat a faerie offering you dinner. Any verbal agreement is treated as binding, and he has a tendency to mumble under his seven coats so you can't always be sure what you are agreeing to. It is a bad idea to borrow books from the Spindleman, because he will inevitably return to request some favour which you will not want to agree to.

The Ancient is older than time, and visits in the dead of winter using her walking frame. She resolutely refuses anything offered her, and it is unclear how she travels to and from the shop each time, because it takes her about thirty minutes to cross the threshold. We have never, not once, managed to give her any meaningful assistance with anything book-related, despite our best efforts.

The Ristlestig is my name for whatever is living in the packing cellars. Amid a sea of crates, boxes, chests and discarded bubble wrap, one can sometimes hear a rustling sound. One might attribute the accompanying chill to a sudden breeze if the cellars weren't so far below street level.

The Suited Gentlemen turn up annually, smartly dressed in matching suits and asking to see any material we have on Ayn Rand. Faces usually obscured by large dark glasses, they move without making a sound, and only travel in pairs.

Sometimes they will bark out a laugh at nothing in particular, as if mimicking what they think humans do.

The temptation is to chase a cryptid away as soon as it appears, but over time you begin to develop a rapport with them. I suspect they consider me as much of a barrier to the enjoyment of the bookshop as I consider them a terrifying esoteric encounter. It's a bit like when people say a spider is as scared of you as you are of it, and you believe them on an objective level, but on an emotional one you still want to scoop it up under a cup and place it outdoors.

The singing cryptid barked a laugh at me, jolting me out of my reverie. She would not sing for me after all, she had decided. I did not have the right aura. Perhaps another time. She drifted over to the shelf containing the modern first editions. No, she was not here to buy a book today, she confirmed, she was just looking.

She left, eventually, holding five empty plastic bags she needed for some undisclosed reason, promising to return.

8

Gourds

I T'S NOT EVERY DAY someone walks through the doors of Sotheran's clutching a dismembered plant carcass, but it happens. The day in question was a quiet and rather sunny afternoon, which in itself should have alerted me that something was about to go awry. The tiny desk, despite my resentment of it, had a few advantages, one of which was being very close to Andrew (who always entertained a variety of interesting and exceptional book runners). On this occasion, the gentleman attempting to hawk his merchandise had the air of a desperate street magician, rattling quickly through several undesirable books before finally reaching the bottom of the proverbial barrel. 'Gourds!' he blurted, revealing his final gambit with a flourish. Andrew's face could have been chiselled on to a lion's body and buried in sand, because he gave no indication whatsoever whether or not this was a winning line of enquiry.

Not to be deterred, the pointy little man unveiled an object from inside the cavernous backpack he'd brought with him. As it was swaddled in bubble wrap it took him a few rather undignified minutes to extract the item from the packaging, before he laid it down with reverence on the desk. He even took a step back to let the sight sink in. Someone, it seemed, had taken one perfectly innocent gourd the size of a basketball, dried the poor thing out and carved into it the face of Queen Victoria. It was as close a likeness as someone could be expected to produce with a machete, which is to say it gurned at me despite facing in the opposite direction. Then, with another swish, he separated the gourd into two halves* to reveal it was hollow, and had a face carved on the other side – some gentleman of past historical significance whose name I never attempted to learn, his legacy reduced

---

* I occasionally refer to the gourd as 'gourds' from hereon out, to reflect its bisected nature.

to scratchings on a piece of shrunken vegetation. You could hang it on the wall, he suggested. A collector's item, certainly. Could any aspiring bookseller afford to let this go?

The sum paid for the demonic gourd was to my mind exorbitant, but Andrew had that look in his eye which suggested there was more to the gourd than it seemed. Did he know something I did not? Was there some secret of gourd-related collectibles to which I was not privy? A world under the surface of book collecting where the wealthy and powerful traded engraved plant matter in an arboreal black market to make the Grand Bazaar blush? After Andrew struck the deal with the moustachioed gentleman, the gourd was acquired for stock, and summarily sealed away in its packaging for cataloguing.

Winters came and went. Customers were solicited for the gourds; seeing them in person caused otherwise enthusiastic patrons to politely but suddenly excuse themselves. The gourds gradually moved from desk to shelf, from shelf to box, and from box to floor, eventually fading out of sight and mind.

Several years later, I stepped on something near my desk, resulting in a loud *crack* which ricocheted through the shop. Already knowing what I would find, I gingerly lifted up my shoe to reveal the scrambled face of Queen Victoria staring up at me accusingly through a cacophony of dust and bubble wrap. She had never made it through the system, trapped in an endless purgatory until my boot ended for ever her dream of finding a new home. Wailing a little internally at how much this might cost me (the broken article was worth more than my paycheque), I gathered up the fragments and attempted to piece them back together, ending up with something that looked almost but not quite entirely unlike Queen Victoria. I briefly considered my options, including surreptitiously squirrelling her out of the shop and dividing the pieces between several different rubbish bins in boroughs across the city, as if I were disposing of a corpse. With a guilty conscience I decided that time would heal all things, and sought out a cupboard I had never seen anyone open, with the faint hope that perhaps I would be dead before the shattered gourd ever saw the light again.

9

Furbishing

RUMMAGING THROUGH THE shelves below ground in search of somewhere to stash the gourds, my hand brushed something wet. Recoiling instinctively (and knocking over a stack of apprentice review paperwork I was sure I had thrown away years ago), I resisted the urge to scream and instead went to find a torch.

Returning to the room now armed with a light source, I delved a little deeper and started to move books aside in the hunt for the culprit. A mottled biography of Dickens. Two botanical primers, courtesy of Mrs Hawthorne. A catalogue of books on magicians (1861–78). Behind it all, as if it had slipped past its shelfmates in an attempt not to be seen, was a green box. Shining the light on it revealed that it hadn't started out green but had been almost entirely overtaken by an invasive species of mould. The infestation didn't seem to have spread to other nearby books, which raised a whole host of questions by itself, but did mean I was able to quickly isolate it using a filthy dishcloth I keep in a drawer in case of ichorous events.* The damp along the back wall had claimed another victim it seemed, but this didn't appear to be a reference book. Someone had gone to the effort of making it a custom case, which suggested that at one point it had been intended for stock, and perhaps had even been made with a specific customer in mind. Feeling a little like the world's most reluctant archaeologist, I used the rag to clean it up a little, revealing a name stamped in gilt on the side: *Edwin Drood*.

Curiosity won out over squeamishness. I opened the box, which folded out to reveal a stack of mouldering blue and white booklets in a state of advanced decay. Alas, it is the curse of all rare booksellers to be able to identify a first edition Dickens from across a dark room, and this was undoubtedly all six issues of his unfinished final novel, *The Mystery of Edwin Drood*. Definitely not an academic reference book. A quick search of the system didn't show it, which meant that it had probably been hanging around in the wrong place for over a decade, until the water rot finally caught up with it. I removed the pages from the box, and, not finding anywhere suitable to store them, wrapped them

---

* 'You should clean the rag, Oliver' you might say to me, but no one ever discovered penicillin by maintaining pristine working conditions.

up in plastic, thinking maybe there was something about them that could be saved. There was really only one person to take them to.

All books might be made equal, but some suffer more than others. When we receive books which have seen better days, we send them downstairs for something called 'furbishing'. It's not quite restoration, and it's not quite cheating – it's something in between. A spry little man called Stephen takes care of our furbishing, and has done since the beginning of time. With a wry smile and a knowing look, he takes on the onerous task of making all the books look as presentable as possible, using an experimental combination of glue, hope and witchcraft. If he's in the office, or if the wind is right, he can be found beneath the stairs under a stack of books trying to mend an errant page or fix an endpaper. He shares this space with the General Secretary, the two of them crammed into the same comfortable nook, where they enjoy a quiet kind of companionship. I've never known him to turn down a task, or say something isn't possible, despite bringing him a number of bibliocorpses over the years.

I always thought it would be rather fun to be a book furbisher, but I don't have the manual dexterity. Furbishing is all about the illusion – about fixing and supporting the book in all the right places while interfering as little as possible. That being said, I once saw him repair a page tear with some artifice that rendered it entirely invisible. I've seen him replace an endpaper entirely with no outward indication that the new one was not the original. You have to admit all these things when you're selling the book, of course, but it still has the reek of sorcery.* How does one become a furbisher? I have no idea. Stephen isn't telling, and no amount of searching online will reveal where they come from. I like to think there's a secret organization which meets every year at some grand conclave, but I'd be just as easily convinced that they simply turn up wherever they're needed, like Mary Poppins. It briefly occurred to me that Stephen might be able to fix the gourds, but I resolved to ask him later once the trail leading to the culprit had gone cold.

If a book really can't be saved by furbishing, because it's in such tatters that there's nothing to work with, but we still need to sell it (perhaps a manuscript, or something signed that has value independent of how it looks), then we'll often try to get it rebound or recased. This involves sending it off to a bookbinder, one of the institutions which takes off book covers and replaces them with leather sourced from special cows, fancy goats, or whatever the client desires. (Before you ask, yes, it is technically possible to bind a book in human leather, but the practice is frowned upon.) Bookbinding is something of a dying art: once very popular, demand has dropped as customers slowly caught on to the idea that the original covers of books were worth preserving. Many bookshops (including Sotheran's) once did the majority of their binding in house. In fact, we had the bookbinding tools until very recently when someone

---

* I have, on more than one occasion, needed to argue with a customer who insisted that a repair had *not* been made, when I had literally seen it done before my eyes.

hawked them to a passer-by, and I suppose it's nice to know they've found purpose somewhere, probably as jousting implements or house decorations. An unpleasant result of the fading of bookbinders is that reliable ones are often unavailable – and when I say reliable ones, I mean ones where you get what you pay for. There's a strange correlation between bookbinders and spontaneous dyslexia when you haggle with them: when you wait eight months for a book to turn up, only to find it titled in fancy gold letters Great Expactions or Little Dorito, you quickly learn to pay the asking price. The waiting list for bookbinding is quite long, and it's a bit like finding a plumber – if a bookbinder is free for work immediately, then one should be cautious.

In very rare cases, the competition for a decent bookbinder reaches fever pitch. I recall a little while back there being an elderly bookbinder (quite famous in his field) who worked well into his nineties. Naturally, as he aged, his availability for work decreased, and demand began to ramp up as people figured out he was soon to shuffle off his mortal coil and pass into whatever realm bookbinders inhabit when they die. A field full of celestial cows they are required to apologize to, perhaps. Anyway, people began to treat the poor old man like a capture-the-flag mission, and I'm fairly sure I heard of someone moving in with him to secure his attentions. Mercifully, he's dead now, so his suffering is over. But I've always considered this some kind of Aesopian warning about never being too good at your job in case you're abducted at the age of ninety and forced to craft books in some ravenous bookseller's dungeon.

Alas, as you might expect, bookbinding is expensive.

Very few books are worth enough to merit it, particularly ones damaged enough that you'd need them rebound in the first place. If a book can't be furbished, and it's not worth enough to rebind? Then that book is in trouble. If such a book ends up in our possession, we sometimes take it down to the Prints department and see if they'd like to break it up into illustrations. We've had some success with this in the past – after all, better to save part of something than none of it, and we can often surgically remove the noteworthy art in a way that preserves it. It's important we do this, because the next step is one no one likes to talk about.

There comes a point where a book isn't worth anything, and you can't save it. You need to throw it away, or recycle it, or (if you have the space) keep it for your own amusement. When I tell people this, they often clutch their pearls and look at me as if I'd suggested we tear down Stonehenge to make way for a supermarket, but the reality of the matter is that a Rare Book Industry survives only because most old books are not worth any money. The nature of our trade is such that the vast majority of antiquarian books aren't worth keeping from a purely financial standpoint. So to make any headway in the book trade, you develop a hard skin early and learn not to listen to the plaintive cries of books as you box them up and donate them to second-hand or charity bookshops.

10

Ballerinas and Ballgowns

I'M NOT SURE who recommended Mr Willoughby to us, but the call came at an inconvenient moment. I was attempting to help the cryptid called Ancient out of the shop, and she was taking an exceptionally long time to cross the threshold, with her walking frame getting stuck at odd angles on every attempt. Whenever I was distracted by another customer, she would somehow disentangle herself from the door and dodder off in another direction complaining that no one would help her leave. This process had been repeating itself for over half an hour when the phone began to screech in the background.

Usually, if I'm doing something else, I'll just leave it and trust that the answerphone is working,* or that the call will ring out. This time it kept ringing over and over until I became so irritated that I abandoned the Ancient in a corner where I could keep an eye on her and stalked over to my desk in a foul mood.

The thing about answering a phone in a bookshop is that if you make the mistake of greeting anyone with anything less than breezy neutrality, the person on the other end invariably decides to make you pay for it. If you work at a bookshop long enough, you have to hone that neutral tone and be ready to adopt it at a moment's notice. Chris is

---

* It won't be – see 11. Proper Apprentice Training.

able to press into service a perfect model of politeness even when he's doing three tasks at once, and James had memorized a list of quicksilver platitudes so practised that for a while you really did believe that whoever he was speaking to was an old friend of his. Alas, I seem to possess a default tone of voice that invites confrontation so I get dragged through the wringer more often than most.

'Good morning,' an elderly voice chirped down the line, though the evidence so far suggested it was nothing of the sort. 'Could I speak to someone about my books?' This is what people say when they are about to launch into a very long explanation, so I sat down to watch the Ancient ram her walking frame vindictively into a bookshelf. He began to talk, and there was no escaping it, because he wanted to give me the story of his life and I don't think he took a single breath for five minutes. There's no way to listen to someone's entire life story without being just a little won over, and soon I was taking down the details of Mr Willoughby, promising I would help with crossed fingers. He worked at a prestigious dance institution as the librarian, he said, and they had many books he'd been commanded to dispose of.

Thinking myself very clever, I passed the buck up the chain. Andrew was experienced in books related to the performing arts, and I informed him that a Mr Willoughby would be by to speak to him about his books. This manoeuvre bought me almost no time at all, because Mr Willoughby was incredibly sprightly for his age (no doubt all that exposure to dancing had rubbed off). Knowing with a pang of guilt that I had caused this, I dodged the encounter by finding something that looked busy on another floor. When enough time had passed that I figured the dust had settled, I emerged, only to find Andrew had kindly arranged for us *both* to see Mr Willoughby again, this time in the belly of the beast. The appointment had been scheduled for the early morning. Which I suppose served me right.

The first clue that the entire enterprise was doomed should have been the building itself, a monstrous glass horror crouching hungrily as if it might reach down and snatch up a pedestrian at any moment. No rare book specialist in their right mind would voluntarily keep a library of rare material in a building made primarily from gigantic sheets of glass; the heat on summer days alone would risk turning the entire collection to twisted, smouldering rags.

When I arrived, I was stopped by a porter in a very expensive-looking suit. He allowed me through only reluctantly, correctly deducing that I was about as far from a dancer as it was possible to be without being wheeled through the doors inside an iron lung. I bolstered my credentials as a bookseller by tripping over the doorstop on the way in.

I was late, of course, and I scurried through the halls trying not to feel intimidated by the walls lined with pictures of elegant people trapped in moments of extreme contortion. You almost felt like their hips were following you as you moved around the room. All of these people were far too busy looking spectacular ever to haunt somewhere as crooked as a rare bookshop.* When I finally found Andrew and Mr Willoughby, my tardiness had given our host a chance to initiate that most dreaded of performances: the backstory. Which I had to listen to for a second time.

When he was ready, we ascended inside a glass lift, a grand statement piece that seemed to exist with the sole purpose of elevating weary travellers about ten feet off the ground. The library nestled in the heart of the building, and Mr Willoughby lured us inside with repeated coaxing. It consisted of a single large room festooned with the kind of heavy-duty shelving you expect in a warehouse. Each shelf was meticulously labelled, partitioned and ordered in a way that softened my heart just a little bit. Framed posters littered the floor.

As he talked, Andrew and I walked about to get a sense of the room. When appraising a library, it's important to do a turn about the place, quietly assess it for notable rarities and establish whether – say, in the event of a hoard of books on exorcism – you need to immediately flee the premises.

The problem presented itself almost instantly, accompanied by a running commentary from the excited Mr Willoughby that also constituted something of a confession. 'I volunteered for this,' he gushed, explaining that no

---

* I have long nursed a belief that people only really have room for one all-consuming hobby in their lives at a time. If you're spending 24/7 in a dance studio, you're not spending it in a basement scrounging about for old books, or knitting.

one else had ever really shown any interest in a dance library. 'It was much smaller when I started,' he continued, regaling us with how he'd pulled it together piece by piece over many years. Left to his own devices, and with no budget whatsoever (forcing him to buy odds and ends using his own money), he'd discreetly collected anything that caught his fancy, straying far and wide from the original brief in the process. Then, he unveiled a series of ballerina dresses, each posed in a lifelike position on a mannequin, which he reminded us were not for sale, but which he wanted to talk about anyway. Each of them had belonged to a famous dead dancer, I heard as I poked about for rarities.

I tried not to catch Andrew's eye as we wandered up and down the stacks, because I already knew what we would find when we looked the books up – the vast majority of them were modern celebrity biographies, reviews of forgotten plays or damaged goods. There wasn't likely any money to be made here at all, at least not enough to justify the time it would take to catalogue them all.

I patiently waited for Andrew to break the bad news to Mr Willoughby, who was grumbling about how he'd been asked to downsize the library and accusing his colleagues of philistinism. Then, Mr Willoughby pulled out a set of binders, in which he'd patiently and painstakingly made a note of exactly how many books were on each shelf, what they were about, what order they were in. To save us time, he said, but the expression on his face told another story entirely. We lost the battle in that moment, truthfully, because Mr Willoughby loved those books. It didn't really matter to him that they weren't worth a single penny. It didn't matter if they were motheaten, or ragged. He'd slowly and surely put the library together himself, and it mattered to him. He couldn't bear the idea of this collection being shoved into recycling, which would probably have been the only reasonable thing to do.

It took me an entire day to pack away all Mr Willoughby's books.* The contents of those carefully organized, meticulously listed shelves were gathered up and collected in a huge van at inordinate expense, and driven across town to the Other Cellars,† where they remain to this day.

11

Proper Apprentice Training

It's HALF PAST FIVE, and one of our customers is desperately trying to teach me long division, to no effect. I'd made the mistake of mentioning in passing that I wasn't very good at maths, by way of small talk. She had taken it as some kind of personal challenge, motivated no doubt by kindness but quickly descending into a powerless sort of despair as I looked blankly at the sheet of numbers the professor had scribbled down in a last-ditch attempt to knock

---

* Andrew mysteriously found somewhere else to be.

† See 34. Dungeoneering.

some sense into me. The closest person who might save me is Chris, who manages the Natural History department, and I think sometimes gets tired of being the smartest person in the room. Of all my colleagues, I think Chris has maybe the most interesting list of clients, and most frequently finds the most expensive books to offer them. I think he has to keep that big brain of his busy somehow, and the only way to do it is to keep as many large plates spinning as possible. Geometry. Microscopes. Evolutionary sciences. The worst part of it is that (as far as I can tell) he created the whole department himself purely because he found an interest in it. I enjoy his company greatly, as he's never without something exciting to show you.

Alas, he is in no mood to intervene with my current issue, because I don't think he wants anyone trying to explain long division to him either. The customer had made what must have been a considerable effort to visit the shop on one of her overseas visits, and I am failing her in a fashion she finds quite extraordinary.

The good news is that this was not the only contribution the bookshop made to my education. Never flush with cash, Andrew had hit upon a cunning scheme in the raising of the latest Sotheran's employee and had enrolled me in the government-sponsored apprenticeship scheme. This would pay some of my wages, as long as Sotheran's could prove they were teaching me a trade. It did not occur to Andrew, I think, that the definition of Apprentice had changed since 1761, and that the scheme was largely intended for plumbers, electricians, hairdressers and other people who serve some practical function in society. Nevertheless, by the time

I had been provided with my tiny desk and a selection of incorrect name badges reading Mike, Peter and John, it was too late in the process to go back.

Shortly after I began work, a well-meaning government-funded Centre for Proper Apprentice Training began to call the shop asking after me. At first I think everyone thought it was a hoax, and duly paid no regard to it, thinking the whole thing might go away if it was ignored long enough. This was not to last.

Eventually, presumably puzzled by the tortured beeping they heard on the phone whenever they tried to call,* other arrangements were made. And so it was that Kylie entered the bookshop, possessed of a bundle of binders, a takeaway coffee, a laptop bag and far too much confidence in the System. She did what everyone does when they enter Sotheran's for the first time, which is freeze and wonder at the deathly silence, before eventually adjusting to the lighting and striking out in search of humans. Introductions were made, and in the absence of anywhere to talk, Kylie and I retreated down to the shadowy nooks of the Catalogue Room, a place for secret meetings if ever there was one.

The meeting did not start well, mostly because James interceded to remove Kylie's coffee, citing it as an

---

* Sotheran's does have an answerphone system, but it has never worked for longer than a day or two. We used to have one which needed resetting overnight – this was one of my responsibilities as an apprentice which I never quite got the hang of, and so I feel a little responsible for our slow devolution into not using one at all. When we replaced the phones the new handsets came with a state-of-the-art answerphone system which was beyond our ability to configure, so the result is the same.

unacceptable risk, and handling it as if it were an unstable
isotope. Once the threat had been removed, we were
granted privacy amid the endless stacks of books shoved
out of sight and mind. Attempts to get her laptop plugged
in resulted in a quest for a plug socket. One was eventually
found in a hidden floor compartment under the table, in
the process of reaching which I knocked open a case, stumbling into a huge metal death mask of Wagner which
chimed with an ironic lingering chord before I could stuff it
back inside and slam the door shut.

By this point, Kylie was looking at me as if she were
trapped in some kind of fever dream. She had the decency
not to pinch herself or run screaming for the door, but I
had the distinct impression this was not what she had signed
up for. Arming herself with her files, she pulled out the
paperwork we needed to go through in order to complete
the apprenticeship. She began to work methodically
through her list. Questions about computers and tills were
met with a shake of the head, or simply 'we don't have that'.
Attempts to explain book cataloguing to her were met with
a justifiably blank expression. She almost broke into pieces
when I tried to explain that I didn't actually know where
the rubbish disappeared to in the evening, so I couldn't be
expected to help out with that. Finally, we reached the end
of the questions. Had I, she asked with a weary sigh, been
shown how to handle customers? She looked so hopeful
that there might be a positive response to this that even as
images flashed through my mind of fending off the Spindleman with a broom, I couldn't bear to disappoint her. Yes, I
assured her. Customers, no problem. Clutching on to this

with renewed, desperate zeal, she seemed to rally. Could I show her?

Returning to the shop floor, it was explained to Andrew (at mortifying length) that Kylie needed to sit back and watch how I handled customers. Finding a stool to perch on, she retreated into the back of the shop, got out a clipboard, and we waited for a customer to walk through the door. Two hours passed, and Kylie slowly seemed to wither under the crushing hope that surely a customer would cross the threshold any moment now. She didn't really seem to know what to say, and I had no words of comfort for her.

Fortunately for myself, and for Kylie, Andrew wrote her a very lovely paragraph or two explaining that everything was fine. Clutching her prize, she took me aside and declared with as much dignity as she could muster that the assessment was concluded, everything was quite satisfactory, and she would be leaving some paperwork to fill out. It was filed where I store all my paperwork, in the wastebin beside my desk, from which it disappeared that evening.

12

Spindleman

HALF PAST THREE in the afternoon, and the Spindleman is gnashing his teeth, spittle flying all over my desk. 'It is worth more than that,' he insists, shuffling about irritably. His eyes are as big as saucers. 'It is worth it. More. More, yes.' He pushes the set of books back across the table to me, as I shake my head and gently try to stop him shoving them into my lap. 'No,' I say in a slow and deliberately calm voice so as not to agitate him further. 'Not for us, not today, thank you.' The Spindleman lets off a noise which is halfway between a curse word and a hiss. 'It is rare,' he chitters. 'No others. No others.' I clean my glasses and try to explain to the Spindleman what the problem is. He's brought in a set of books which together comprise a catalogue detailing the exact specifics of a particular historical set of porcelain. They are exceedingly heavy.

I lay the books out. 'Yes,' I concede, 'they are hard to find.' The Spindleman crows a little, and does the little hop to the other leg he does when he thinks he has secured a victory.

The first and most obvious hurdle is that in order for someone to care about your rare book, it has to be scarce. Hard to find. People are paying you, as a rare bookseller, to locate things they might not otherwise be able to get their hands on. Part of why you can charge them a suitably high price is your ability to give them an arch expression and suggest they 'find another'.* On some level, people who bring us books to sell understand this part of the business and how it works. If you can find loads of copies on the market, then you can't ask as much as you would like. It's actually quite easy to find a rare book, if that's all you care about – statistically speaking, most books are rare once you start digging around in the detritus of the twentieth century.

---

* This was one of James's favourite pastimes.

'But that's not the only thing that matters, is it?' I continue. He tips his head with a scowl, knowing what I am about to say before I say it. The Spindleman is long in the tooth, and was hoping to slip these books by a less experienced member of staff. 'If you look here,' I say, turning the books over, 'there's damage to the spine, no? And fading. They're not in good shape.'

The part that starts to trip people up is the need for the book to be in good condition. A supplier might bring in a copy of *The History of the Adventures of Joseph Andrews*, and I'll get very excited only to discover that it is missing the second plate (which should show Fanny fainting at some bad news).* In an instant, it goes from a book that could be worth thousands of pounds to being worth absolutely nothing.

People often think of a book's condition as a linear sliding scale of value, but it's far more complicated than that. A book in fine condition is worth a premium, and it's not true that a book which is half as nice will fetch half the price. It's more likely to be simply worthless. (Remember: 'good' = on fire.) Booksellers can argue about the reasons for this until the cows come home, but it's an industry of collectors and those collectors are governed by many of the

---

* I have a soft spot for Henry Fielding's *The History of the Adventures of Joseph Andrews and of his Friend Mr Abraham Adams*, not only because it is one of the earliest novels in the English language (which it is), or because it was written entirely to lampoon other writers of the period (which it was), but because it contains the characters Lord and Lady Booby, who are usually illustrated rather ungenerously in plates, and because Fanny can't seem to stop getting kidnapped. Early editions of it become quite complicated, as it was frequently pirated, but I never object to seeing it.

same principles of collectors in other fields – they want the best version possible of the item they're buying. It seems particularly important for books, where you can only rarely expect to own the *only* copy, but you might be able to find the *nicest* one. In short, many books always have to be much closer to pristine condition than you'd think before anyone will be confident enough to buy them from you.

The Spindleman sulks a little, but he has not come unprepared. 'As good as it gets,' he says, and I know that perhaps he is right. It's possible this set of books often appears in a similar condition, which means he has me cornered. I have one last requirement up my sleeve, however, and he isn't going to like it, particularly as he's already started to divest his cart of similar books all over my workspace.

I stop him offloading by placing a hand in the way. I don't touch him. That would be unwise. 'I think the real problem is . . .' I begin, trying to find the right words to express the golden rule at the heart of all bookselling. What you try not to tell people, because no one ever wants to hear it, even though it really is the simplest reason a book might not be worth any money, even if it's as scarce as hen's teeth and in perfect condition. A completely subjective variable, utterly in the power of the bookseller to decide, against which there really isn't any arguing. 'Look here,' I say to the Spindleman, as his expression grows flinty, 'I just don't think anyone *cares* about these books.'

Later that afternoon, we find ourselves reading a long complaint letter from the Spindleman, who takes a page and a half to explain exactly why he is dissatisfied with our service, and goes to great pains to assure us that he will never return.* My worries are put to rest when I am told that offending the Spindleman is a rite of passage.

13

James and the Giant Midden

RUBBISH IS ONE of those things you don't think about much until circumstance forces your hand. Cast your mind back a little while to a frantic Oliver holding a shattered gourd, guiltily contemplating what to do with it, or a rather cross Oliver holding a stack of useless apprenticeship paperwork. The sensible thing to do, surely, would be to hide all of it in the bin and wait for nature to take its course. Things were not so simple at Sotheran's, however, where the bins acted less as waste disposal and more as a generalized redistribution system.

I first noticed the phenomenon when attempting to dispose of a faulty stapler. James disapproved of staplers in general, as a rogue staple left inside a book can result in all kinds of bizarre oxidization. I had been provided with one nevertheless, inside one of the tiny drawers in the tiny desk, and quickly discovered that it was inoperable. Some quirk of the catch inside it caused it (instead of securing two

---

* He will.

pieces of paper together as intended) to fire off loose staples into the air in random directions. I attributed its presence among my stationery to be some oversight, as it was not the only highly suspect piece of equipment left in the diminutive workspace by my predecessor, a list including but not limited to: a rusty letter opener, an ambiguous tool with an ivory hilt (purpose unknown to this day), a dusty floppy disk and an entire case of colourful needlework pins.

I did the only sensible thing and consigned the stapler to the waste paper bin. It had not occurred to me, prior to this, to wonder where all the rubbish went in the evenings, but the next morning I began to have reason for curiosity, as the stapler had returned itself to my drawer. Initially discounting it as a trick of memory, I repeatedly attempted to dispose of the stapler in the aforementioned receptacle, only to find myself in a Groundhog Day scenario where the possessed device would endlessly manifest somewhere within my workstation the next morning without fail. I began to rid myself of it further afield, placing it in various bins around the shop in the hope that if I put enough distance between me and the stapler, it might not be able to find its way home. No such luck. No matter the contrivance, I was unable to throw it away without it returning like a boomerang.

It wasn't just the stapler that proved hard to jettison. Scrap papers inveigled themselves mysteriously back into piles and on to desks. Pamphlets and leaflets snuck into folders unnoticed. Wires and defunct technology crept into boxes, found by accident several months after the fact. Enough was, eventually, enough. Working up the courage to ask a question I might not like the answer to, I decided to go and get the answer from the horse's mouth, and went down to the little office under the stairs where Evelyn toiled away at the never-ending cycle of numbers and letters that kept us afloat. 'We have a cleaner,' she explained, diplomatically, as if that were enough by itself. This was the first I was hearing of it, and it raised some other questions about the dust levels in the shop which I decided to shelve for a later date. No other justification was forthcoming, and Evelyn considered the matter concluded. Besides, it was pointed out to me that there was a strange lady threatening to sing on the upper floor, and shouldn't I be dealing with that instead of worrying about missing staplers?

The enigma was solved months later due to a particularly tenacious customer who kept me late at the shop. Arriving at closing time (and slipping under the grate to worm his way in), he had decided that today was the day he wanted to look at all the books on the top shelf at the back of the shop, but only one at a time. He would not cross the shop floor to get closer to the shelf, mind, requiring me to bring the books to him one by one. Every other staff member had retreated into the night by this point, shooting me apologetic looks as they fled. All apart from James. He often stayed late, this I knew, legend had it sometimes into the small hours. As I ferried dated picture books back and forth for the intrusive gentleman customer ('Nostalgia! Perfection!' he burbled, frothing just a little) I began to see James ferreting about the shop. There was something circumspect about his movements. Discreetly, I began to watch as he went from desk to desk, peering in the wastebins and carefully removing what was inside, performing what appeared to be a brief inventory of the contents. Certain items were isolated and reverently restored to the shop floor, tucked away in crannies, or grimly sequestered out of sight. He had the decency to look just a little abashed, performing this task in the open, but this unfamiliar emotion was not significant enough for him to avert his course.

I was transfixed by this process, enough that I stopped paying much attention to Intrusive Gentleman, who by this point had lost himself in *The Tale of Squirrel Nutkin*. Gradually, a set of rubbish was assembled which James found unworthy of rescue, and deposited in a black sack like the work of some twisted Krampus. With dour countenance, as if levying a capital punishment on the detritus, he strapped it to his bike.* Lashed to the back by complex artifice, this finally seemed to satisfy him, and he creaked away into the night with the offending black bag firmly under his watchful eye.

The next morning, I gently raised the matter with some of my colleagues, thinking that perhaps the subtle hand of peer pressure might be marshalled in favour of common sense. The understanding dawned on me that everyone else already knew this was occurring to one degree or another, and had either resolved to live with it or subconsciously adjusted their habits to account for it.

---

* How to describe James's bike? To its credit, it did have two wheels, neither of which I suspect originated from bicycles. In general, it gave the impression of having been replaced piece by piece, like Theseus's ship, until not a shred of the original framework remained. Straps of plastic and paper were loosely attached or entangled in the sprockets and basket, artfully concealing whatever James was carrying.

14

Diderot and Disability

I F JAMES WAS possessed of strange and furtive habits after hours, he remained energetic in the daylight. As time passed, I became aware that Sotheran's had not entertained an apprentice (at least, not in a formal capacity) for as long as anyone could remember. My predecessors had all been ambitious individuals, the kind of people your aunt might have said were Going Places, hired as full-time staff but quickly moving on to other situations. Some of them had experience in the trade of antiques and rare books already, and many of them possessed degrees and other qualifications which I presume they were able to leverage for tasks that suited their temperaments. By comparison, my status as an apprentice put me in a position where I was bottom of the food chain.* No degree, no aspirations. Just me, a wonky tape measure and whatever tutelage my colleagues saw fit to provide. To their credit, everyone saw this as partially their responsibility – they say it takes a village to raise a child, and perhaps it takes an entire shop to train a bookseller. As part of his contribution to this communal effort, James liked to make sure I always had an activity to keep my hands busy. Usually this involved some grand scheme

---

* Those who had occupied the front desk before me had all achieved their own version of success, either by inventing some technological wonder, moving to a full-time bookseller role at another shop, or generally using Sotheran's as a springboard to loftier heights.

he felt unable (or unwilling) to enact on his own, and I got the distinct impression that he had been waiting for the opportunity to indulge himself in these exercises for some time, restraining himself only for lack of a willing accomplice, a role to which I was elevated as a matter of expediency.

It was during the handling of the Diderot encyclopaedia that I started to notice something was wrong. Some years earlier, the shop had managed to get their hands on a set of the *Encyclopédie* produced by Denis Diderot between 1751 and 1772. A gigantic undertaking of Enlightenment-adjacent optimism, the book ran to a total of seventeen enormous volumes filled with just about everything the layman could want to know about anything. Alas, when Sotheran's acquired the volumes, some of them had already met terrible fates at the hands of time, damp and night creatures, so the decision was made to divide and conquer, splitting the plates and pages up into collections. A few on needlework. Some on lobsters. A little on spectacles. The collection took up a vast number of folders, each of which was crammed with a very specific list of pages cannibalized from the various volumes in a particular order, and exhaustively catalogued by my predecessor (who, I discovered, was a stickler for detail). It was decreed a few months into my apprenticeship that I should double-check these records, make sure everything was in order. Simple enough, though it might take a while. For some peace and quiet I tucked myself away in the Catalogue Room with my task, and began to leaf through it.

Now, I have a slight confession to make. Prior to my

time at Sotheran's I had not always been what one might call a model employee. In all those engagements I'd developed a reputation for being a bit sleepy, absent-minded, or otherwise not up to speed with current events.* So much so that I'd had to jump swiftly from my last job before I was pushed – a rather unpleasant experience that I was loath to repeat. I'd always assumed that it was the high-paced nature of the jobs which caused my fatigue, and that everyone else was dealing with the same feelings. It was as I sat in possibly the least fatiguing job in the world and felt a wave of sleepiness wash over me that I figured out something was in fact dreadfully wrong.

No matter which way you looked at it, there was no way that sitting about leafing through pages should be wearing me out as quickly as it was. As time went by, I began to experience the familiar symptoms which had cost me my job in the past – bleary moments, napping at the desk, repeatedly walking into a wall like a chicken without its head. Ordinarily, by the three-month mark this would have resulted in several talks with a manager-type, who would firmly insist that I cease my late-night activities and take my working responsibilities seriously, despite my protestations that I did not really have a social life, on account of all the time I spent asleep. This would then lead into further talks about making an effort, some official censures, and then finally my slinking

---

* I am mortified to this very day by my short, abortive role as a legal apprentice where I misfiled a piece of critical paperwork and the case got to the high court before everyone in the room suddenly realized in the exact same moment that the entire case was based on a clerical mistake. My clerical mistake.

off into the dark never to be seen again, unable to figure out why I couldn't keep up with my colleagues.

Worst of all, reading for any length of time sent me right into dreamland with alarming regularity, and reading was understandably part of the job at Sotheran's. I would jerk to a start at my desk several times a day in a fluster of embarrassment. Time continued to pass in this manner, and similar incidents came and went without particular comment. On one occasion I attended an auction and dozed off in the middle, dropping whatever I was holding. Still, no reprimand.

I entertained an entire year on the edge of conscious-ness, operating in fits of activity and sudden lethargy, and still no one had said a thing. In previous jobs, this ten-dency had been remarked upon in less than a week, and I'd been out of the door as soon as they could legally manage it. My desk was two metres from the managing director's, but Andrew seemed to consider my tiredness none of his business, or at least not of enough significance that he was prepared to make an issue of it. I've often wondered why, and perhaps it was because most of the Sotheran's staff were struggling with ailments of their own, and were trusted to deal with them in whatever manner befitted them and afforded them some measure of dignity in doing so.*

If Andrew noticed any difference in my temperament

---

* For instance, Andrew had rather infamously put his back out as a young bookseller picking up a box of Trollopes, and he frequently disappeared to have his back treated as a result.

after my diagnosis of narcolepsy (and after I acquired some medicine to help me stay awake), he never said. In retrospect, I have come to believe that the soporific nature of the bookshop served to camouflage the problem until I was able to address it. Even with the medical help, I remain a slower person than most, drifting from task to task in a stately manner.

It took me two weeks to sort the Diderot plates into their sections and check them against the notes left by one of my predecessors, a 'Mike' I have never met and who produced incredibly detailed catalogue descriptions. I think it was at this point when I realized that I would be given the benefit of the doubt when it came to completing my own work. However long it took was however long it needed to take, and no questions were asked. I'd struggled my entire life with people assuming that I was lazy, or deliberately skiving, and the implicit trust I received without even having to ask for it was worth more than a thousand Diderot plates.

15

An Experiment in Biochemistry

THE MAN WALKED in carrying a large box under one arm. He'd chosen a bad time of day, firmly in the post meridiem slump, and so it was the tireless James who went over to figure out how to turn him around as quickly as possible. They talked for a little while in the shadows before I was called over. I approached, but cautiously – I had not forgotten the time James had uncovered an old bust of Churchill, only to discover it was home to a hive of biting insects which drove everyone out of the shop.

The visitor had brought in a thin leather-bound tome they wanted to sell, something of a family heirloom. Inside was a yellowing copy of *Measure for Measure*. Printed in 1623, the play had clearly been extracted from what is commonly known as the First Folio, an incredibly rare book which is the only reliable source for about twenty of Shakespeare's plays. Only 750 were ever printed, and of those only a few hundred are accounted for in private collections and institutions. As a bookseller, you don't really get to see something this scarce and influential in the wild very often – most copies of books like this have already been located and bought by people who are unlikely ever to let them go. Even though it had been separated from the rest of the text, it gave us something to coo over, as if someone had brought a baby into the shop.*

As one can imagine, a text like this would set the shop back a large amount of money to acquire, and so some due diligence was required. It is a rare enough item that Sotheran's has even sold single leaves from the same book as rather expensive wall decorations. The owner left the play with us to inspect, and went about his day, confident that he'd soon be in possession of a rather large cheque. Back at the shop, we loomed over the book as a routine (and careful)

---

* Actually bringing a baby into the shop would have produced less awe, and instead a number of pointed suggestions that perhaps it was time to bite the bullet and finally teach the little one how to read.

inspection was performed, checking for missing pages, peculiar colouring, odd printing techniques, anything that might indicate a forgery. As we studied it, a light came on in James's eyes and he rushed back to his desk to dig around for something. He returned a moment later wielding a small torch that he explained was ultraviolet. He turned it on. Sometimes, he continued, you can use UV to discern where mechanical or chemical repairs have been made to paper. I was already staring at the title page of the book, where the purple light had discovered a horror story. The cold light of truth informed anyone who cared to look that the book had not only borne witness to a litany of sins, but that some of the paper had been rather cleverly repaired. The light revealed in stark detail where the different papers had been fused together, in a way imperceptible to the naked eye. The UV light was slowly turned off, and never mentioned again, but the book was nevertheless taken into stock (James did not seem unduly fazed by damage that could only be reliably witnessed by someone carrying about a magic wand) and a cataloguing note was crafted pointing out that some 'restoration' had taken place.

As my apprenticeship continued, excuses were found to bring me more complicated kinds of books. Older things with more peculiar bindings, strange pasts and odd provenances. The logic was that I should become more familiar with obscure terms, but I also think the others loved to show off their new acquisitions (and I had no complaints there). A book furnished with a tail made from goat hair. A bible smaller than a penny.

Frequently, Georg would approach me holding some

bizarre object in both hands, with the question 'What is unusual about this?' The correct response was usually completely beyond me, and after a few moments of inspection during which I pretended to have a snowball's chance in hell of guessing the answer, I would gracefully admit defeat. Georg has a particular gift for detail, and frequently pinpoints irregularities that other people might miss. Not a week passes by when he doesn't come up to the shop floor to show me something esoteric, unfolding a gigantic map like a concertina, or pointing out a forgery only discernible due to the faintest of pixellations visible through his trapezoid magnifying glass.

I have yet to provide a satisfactory answer to any of these impromptu challenges, despite the many opportunities given, but the repeated failures are more than compensated for by the opportunity to listen to the explanation. The truth of the matter is that bookselling is the ugly stepchild of the antiques business or the art world, and our shelves are filled with a great many fascinating and peculiar articles that go entirely unremarked on by visitors, unless we go to great effort to point them out.

Early one morning, which is to say about five minutes before noon, Rebekah (who diligently manages our modern firsts and literature with a leave-no-stone-unturned attitude quite out of character for a bookseller) politely sent around a note asking whether anyone knew if a certain book was *still* poisoned. It transpired that Georg had identified a subsection of his stock as being impregnated with a mildly aggressive toxin designed to kill insects, and one of these had made it all the way from some far-flung collection on to a shelf and thence into a sales catalogue. The book had originally been intended for sale in a humid climate, and some bright spark had engineered this as an ambitious and amusingly short-sighted solution to book-eating bugs that rendered the tome useless to anyone not wearing leather gloves. The toxicity of the binding was noted in a footnote at the very bottom of the description, with the same airy tone one might deploy when talking about the weather. It was, in fact, the very last thing one might see when handling the book, which might prove unfortunate for anyone who didn't read the entire description before picking it up. Ordinarily I might have left this alone as Someone Else's Problem, but the image haunted my mind of being found at the bottom of a staircase, my skeleton clutching a poisoned book, and so a tentative email was sent up the chain, resulting in a sweep of the system for more contaminated books.* We turned up seven before the search was exhausted, six of which were isolated and one of which has gone rogue.

On the other end of the scale, one needn't only be vigilant for books which could kill you, but also for those which are illegal. As a whimsical counterpoint to Georg's cavalier attitude to death, James would take a wicked glee in teaching me about the various ways in which a book dealer can evade the grasp of the law. The instance which sticks in my mind most firmly was when he brought over a small prayer

---

* A word of advice, if you value your life: stay away from any virulently bright green cloth bindings from the Victorian period, because the wretched things were coloured using arsenic, and it's a nasty way to go.

book bound in a macabre white substance that reminded me of bone. Celluloid, he assured me, with a stage wink that implied some kind of private joke to which I was not party. Much later, I discovered that in certain circles it is traditional to describe fake ivory as celluloid (also 'French Ivory' or 'Ivorine'), because trading any book bound in ivory is banned, so to refer to it at all would be in bad taste and risk it being seized by a customs officer with no grasp of nuance. To this day, I still overhear people describing books as having a 'celluloid' binding with an arch expression. Similarly, one tries not to acknowledge the wide and disturbing array of materials in which it is possible to bind a book. Rebekah, I gather, has some knowledge of anthropodermic bibliopegy, or books bound in human skin,* but this is not the kind of thing that Sotheran's would court. Not all books are suitable for the shelves. How would one even fill out the export forms? Human remains, lightly foxed?

16

Curiosa and Curiosa

ONE OF THE many unwritten rules of rare bookselling is that the more effort you put into helping someone, the more likely that person is to deliberately inconvenience

---

* Purely academic, I am assured.

you in the long run. So it was with the Mariner who entered the shop dragging behind him a suspicious portfolio. Small and wiry, with a haunted (and somehow nautical) look that seemed to stare right over your shoulder at all times, he made his way carefully into the shop, wending past other staff members who sensed the danger and fled the scene.

In one of those casual decisions that changes your life permanently, I engaged him, hoping that whatever he wanted would be outside my limited area of expertise (and that I would be able to get back to my book). With a smile that did not reach his eyes, he began to shed books everywhere, in a determined fashion that didn't brook argument. As he did so, he launched into a breathless diatribe about how important these incunabula were, how vital, how *magnificent*. It took four polite attempts to interrupt him before I finally got him to stop unpacking and explain what he wanted. Mercifully, the pack of decidedly-not-incunabula which he wanted to hawk didn't seem like the kind of thing I would be chastised for turning away, so I gently turned him around with a view to getting him off my plate and out of the premises as quickly as possible. He gave me another one of his bone-chilling glares, and it became clear that he wasn't going anywhere until he was ready. He decided, with admirable certitude, that my objective assessment of his goods as 'not for us' could be changed if only it were set within the context of his lifelong travails.*

---

* This tactic is not an uncommon one, designed to exhaust the bookseller emotionally until they give you money to go away. It's time-honoured because it works.

The upper floor being suddenly mysteriously empty of anyone who could save me, I was subjected to longwinded (though admittedly entertaining) excerpts from his life, which painted him as a devoted mariner on shore leave from some distant frontline and selling treasures acquired on his travels to assure a comfortable retirement. I was not yet at the stage in my bookseller apotheosis where I was willing to be rude to assure myself an exit, so I ended up listening until he had finished, at which point he left, loudly declaiming bookshops to be better than therapy and vowing fiercely to return.

Some months passed, and I began to think that perhaps I had imagined the encounter. This turned out to be wishful thinking.

The Mariner returned with a large suitcase. It contained an assortment of sea-adjacent tools such as a compass and a collection of damp shells. 'Don't worry,' he barked at me as he parked himself yet again in front of my desk, 'you're in no danger from me, lad.' I had not considered that I might be until that moment, and now I couldn't stop thinking about it. If it were possible, the Mariner had gained more personality in his absence, and he now wore an eyepatch. If I'd been inclined to give him time before, then I was now held emotionally hostage. He fanned out his offerings with a spark of hope in his one working eye that I already knew I would be too weak to extinguish. One by one he offered books that I couldn't take from him. A coverless book on bowel movements? No. A ragged Dickens? I am afraid not. At the very bottom of his bag, something golden glimmered, and he finally picked it out as if he had saved the very best for last.* My eyes locked on to it with desperation, because I wasn't emotionally ready for another round of war stories, and it had occurred to me that perhaps if I bought something then he would leave promptly. A sacrifice to the sea god in return for leniency.

As he passed this final book to me, he assured me that his second in command had been through it page by page to check it was complete. It had, he continued, been passed around his friends and acquaintances so they could all check it, just to be sure. It soon became very clear why, because a casual peep inside revealed a motley array of erotic photographs.

Now, Sotheran's is no stranger to the odd salacious item. In fact, it's quite common in the trade for many general book dealers to host at least a few items in their collection which they might keep on a high shelf, in a concealed cupboard, or inside a glass case that they never dust. They come by Sotheran's from time to time, either as part of a larger collection or because they're important in their own right. One becomes rather sanguine about it after a while, because there is no point in human history when people weren't producing rude books, and more importantly some of them are worth a great deal of money. As a rule of thumb, if you're looking for naked people that a book dealer wants you to find, then search for Erotica. If

---

* Booksellers and collectors adore shiny covers. There's a particular book, *The Savoy Cocktail Book*, which (aside from being an art deco masterpiece) is hunted because of its silver plumage. You can almost guarantee that antiquated shinies will light an avaricious fire in the belly of most booksellers.

you're looking for some that a dealer is trying artfully to conceal, then search for Curiosa. If you get too deep into the rare book world, you'll also find it untagged in lots of places where the dealer simply didn't find it noteworthy enough to mention, or if the dealer in question considered it Fine Art, a distinction which might still hold some dying ember of meaning in art galleries or higher institutions of learning but to book dealers seems to depend entirely on personal idiosyncrasy. In truth, if you intend to wander the world of rare books, you won't often find dealers making a significant distinction between what a modern author might consider adult content and everything else. On the shelves of Sotheran's you'll find *Wind in the Willows* sat alongside the adventures of Viscountess Vane, legendary eighteenth-century widow with a hundred lovers. Hokusai's various lovemaking couples are displayed alongside his landscapes. I think booksellers are simply less interested in arcane discussions of whether or not a particular item constitutes pornography, and more in how long it takes to sell so they can feverishly buy another book with the money.

That being said, if you do stumble across anachronistic or seemingly gratuitous decorative erotica in the book trade, then nine times out of ten it will be of a woman, specifically the special kind of anatomically convoluted and eerily inaccurate woman designed for men who are beyond caring if it is a faithful likeness or not.* A young and

---

* The strangely pervasive presumption that all booksellers are both male and straight made itself rudely apparent to me when a distant colleague from another bookshop with too much time on his hands and no sense of

unsuspecting Oliver discovered more examples than he would have liked in places he did not expect, which I like to think makes me something of an expert in heavily distorted eroticism. Usually it's a case of some determined book-binder with a lot of enthusiasm but a laissez-faire grasp of what humans actually look like stamping a series of golden breasts (the appropriate collective noun eludes me, but it was quite the artistic jumble) on to a fancy leather binding, and I have to say it seems rather unfair to me that I have never once been surprised by a gilded phallus.

The book offered by the Mariner was filled with pictures of scantily clad women posing for the camera, which seemed mundane enough at first, though as one flicked through the book the tools and poses given to the models took on more and more of a frantic nature. French maid outfits were soon replaced by lumberjack uniforms or cowboy get-ups, diving helmets and an increasingly strange array of devices pre-sumably erotic to the magazine's readers but completely opaque to me. By the time the models started threatening each other with firearms and enacting sapphic romances I had already decided that We Must Have It.

My enthusiasm for this must have leaked out into the universe, which in quick succession decided to offer me a history of flagellation, a vintage lingerie catalogue, and a host of other quite disreputable items which almost immediately

---

boundaries attempted to 'reward' me for some task well done with some images from his personal collection. It was almost certainly some form of workplace harassment, but I was particularly irritated that it didn't even *occur* to him that I might prefer a different kind of smut.

sold and found new owners. This period of my bookselling career has since been referred to as 'Oliver's smut phase', and I have no regrets whatsoever.

17

The Big Money

I'M STANDING ON a train platform, and my contact is late for our scheduled meeting. I'm cradling a large package in my arms, which I have lugged all the way from Sotheran's down into this subterranean hellscape. I've never met the client before, as we've only communicated on the phone through his butler, a reedy-voiced man of few words. The client, unnamed, has ordered several books on the occult, which he demanded be wrapped discreetly in brown paper and ferried to a drop-off point by hand. And so, here I am, waiting on a filthy underground platform holding a stack of expensive books, looking from left to right in the hope that the manservant will appear before I need to put the books on the platform floor. The police on the underground have been carrying rather large guns in recent days, and the ones at Oxford Circus like to follow me around ever since I made the mistake of referring to myself as a 'dealer' within earshot. The exchange is performed in a series of hurried whispers when I find my contact standing in a dimly lit alcove at the end of the platform. He's clutching his thick overcoat around him as if he's trying to conceal something, and he takes the books with barely a word, neatly packing them into his briefcase. With our business concluded, I look at my pocket watch. It's stopped, because I forget to wind it sometimes, but I already know I'm late for my next meeting.

The first time I tried to take a four-figure payment from someone, for a lavish set of Austen trussed up in red leather, my heart almost stopped in my chest. They'd sauntered in looking for a gift, which to my mind meant perhaps a negligently selected potted plant and a hastily written card, not a month's pay. I didn't grow up around a great deal of money, and spending all day being responsible for a host of books collectively worth more than I would make in my entire career was initially nerve-racking. The tension of attempting to casually run several thousand pounds through an ancient card machine cannot be overstated, and the notion that I might accidentally slip and move the decimal point one way or the other still causes me to wake up in the dead of night and reach for my emotional support folio.

Items worth eye-watering amounts of money are always stashed in secret places, though it's common for rare bookshops to store items priced in the thousands near the counter in glass cabinets so someone can always keep an eye on them. Richer bookshops than Sotheran's can keep stockpiles of expensive books out of sight and mind, pulling them out of their sleeves like rabbits from a hat whenever the need presents itself. The rest of us have to pick and choose which expensive items we buy quite carefully, because if we can't sell it, then it's just a very expensive slab of tree. It's only worth thousands of pounds if someone will buy it for that, after all. Further, there's a phenomenon peculiar to rare bookshops, in that the longer you keep an expensive item, the less likely you are ever to get rid of it. It sticks in the mind of your customers, and the common wisdom is that the more often a customer sees a particular item, the more they begin to think that something must be wrong with it, or that perhaps it isn't that desirable after all. They say that a new car begins to lose value as soon as you drive it out of the showroom, but a rare book starts to lose value the moment you put it on the shelf. It only occurs to me now that this might be the reason we're so vulnerable to hagglers and bargain hunters: in our heart of hearts, we know that making a little money on a book is better than leaving it there to slowly become a dead albatross in a fancy cabinet.

That being the case, when a staff member brings in a book worth a significant amount of money, they're expected to have a *plan*. Some idea of what they intend to do with it, from start to finish. If Chris (our custodian of books on the sciences) acquires a gigantic book of skeletons by Vesalius, the founder of modern anatomy, it doesn't matter if he's spent the last forty-eight hours on a round trip to France to snatch it from the clutches of a glamorous Siberian heiress, he has to get on with selling it or watch a book worth £90,000 when it entered the shop slowly tick down to being worth a fraction of what he paid for it. The more the book is worth, the more intense the pressure, which is why I have an incredibly hard time making high-value purchases – I simply can't bear the crushing weight of expectation on my shoulders. And the book trade is a fickle place; it doesn't take much to ruin your prospects.

A good example of this going wrong is a copy of *Casino Royale* which we had in stock for years. We intended to sell the book for tens of thousands of pounds, so you can guess how much we must have paid for it. A heart-stopping amount of money. The valuable thing about this particular book was that Ian Fleming had signed it, which was highly unusual for what was already a very scarce book. We had some paperwork tracing the provenance, and a guarantee from a fellow book dealer (an expert in this area) that the signature was real. Cast iron, surely. Alas, dealing with books with staggering price tags means that news travels at an alarming rate throughout the entire trade if there is gossip to be had. It didn't take long before somehow the rumour arose that the signature was fake, and suddenly the book was unsaleable. Bookselling is a confidence game, gossip spreads fast, and even a little doubt was enough to throw off the potential sales that had been lined up for it.* The book had to be sidelined and put away until the rumours faded.

Things get very strange and surreal when you are

---

* If you've ever tried to get a signature verified, you'll know how impossible it is. Signature experts we've contacted in the past have made it very clear to us that they aren't able to confirm anything for certain, and that they really are only giving us their best guess, which when you're trying to put minds at ease is not massively helpful.

talking about vast sums of money. When you reach art gallery levels of expenditure, you find that the customers aren't always even concerned about owning the book. The purchase is more of a statement. Sotheran's has, for a long time, owned the estate of famous bird illustrator John Gould, bought after his death in the nineteenth century. The vast stacks of precious bird prints were moved from basement to basement for over a hundred years until it was decided that we should probably do something with them,* and years were spent finding someone who could afford the astronomical sum of money they were worth. They were, in the end, bought by someone who if I remember correctly immediately donated them to a library. I think the library put his name on a wing, which was rather taxonomically clever of them.

As one of the younger booksellers, I keep my eyes firmly on the floor where they belong. This doesn't result in any great feats of salesmanship, but it does mean that I get to walk around without my heart lodged in my throat. I think in order to be a really successful book dealer you probably have to have a gambler's spirit, but I think I'd much rather be moderately successful than suffer the kind of scrutiny placed on the spectacular.

---

* There was a period when the Packing department were using some of them as a card table.

18

The Sotheran Curse

ANY RESPECTABLE OLD bookshop comes with a few mysteries and curses baked into the foundations. The Sotheran history starts all the way back in the early 1760s, when the first Sotheran to open a bookshop decided he no longer wanted to be an apothecary, and bought up the stock of a retired book dealer with a partner called Todd. No sooner had they gone into business together in York than Todd and Sotheran got into a row, the nature of which has not survived to the present day, but which was acrimonious enough that the company biographer was able to trace the silhouette of it some centuries later.* Following that, a London branch opened when one of the Sotheran heirs got into some kind of nebulous trouble and needed to be relocated to the other side of the country.

Fast forward a hundred years or so, and the last Henry Sotheran was hit by a tram on Piccadilly as he stepped out of the shop (or so the story goes). Various news clippings from the time tell slightly different stories: some say he was roaring drunk, others that it was a car. The nuances vary with each telling, but they all agree that he didn't die far from the bookshop, which perhaps explains why his ghost lingers here.

---

* For the complete company history, which I would not describe as light reading but is very comprehensive, see *Bookmen* by Victor Gray.

As malevolent spirits go, Henry isn't completely unreasonable. He hasn't killed anyone as far as we know, and he doesn't stage gas leaks or write unnerving things on the bathroom mirrors. No, Henry is a ghost with manners, even if he's prone to the odd tantrum. So it is to Henry that all unexplained events are attributed, such as books hurling themselves from shelves when no one is present. Precisely what causes the fits of pique which result in locked cases creaking open and pages fluttering all over the place is unclear, though his pointedly consistent manifestations suggest he looks uncharitably on just about all our decisions.

We keep portraits of two notable Sotherans above the stairwell. I was told their names were Thomas and Maria, some pivotal crux of the Sotheran dynasty now reduced to dusty memories. Thomas has a rather arch expression, and Maria looks thoroughly sick of him. It used to be the case that they were kept in the cellars away from each other, but these days they've been restored to the upper floors so they can judge everyone coming through on their appearances. I rather think they like it there. However disagreeable they find their current fate, they would no doubt be forced to agree that it constitutes a better memorial than the only other Sotheran monument: a small and rather ignoble sink built into the wall of the church across the street and dedicated to their daughter-in-law Rosetta, into which pigeons like to defecate.

Every old bookshop develops a ghost or two in time, I like to think. I recall one of our competitors used to own a building in Berkeley Square which housed a fairly famous ghost that liked to scream and drive people mad. They never did quite live down the reputation for sharing their premises with a homicidal spirit. All in all, I feel rather fortunate that we ended up with a quiet one who is satisfied with a few antisocial gestures – even more so now that he has decided to stop rattling the pipes for an hour whenever anyone goes to the bathroom.

For all that Henry seems an amenable tenant, he is (or so the common wisdom tells us) the reason Sotheran's has enjoyed a turbulent financial history over the years,[*] and the reason cursed books seem to gravitate towards us. In recent years his ire has abated somewhat, which I attribute to us moving the portraits of Thomas and his wife from the cellars to pride of place above the stairwell, in the wake of which the finances demonstrably improved.

The Sotheran tradition of cursed books begins with *The Rubaiyat of Omar Khayyam*. This is the name given to the English translation of a selection of quatrains attributed to Omar Khayyam, known as 'the Astronomer-Poet of Persia'. This book is one of those texts which has been republished more times than anyone cares to count – some collectors boast entire libraries consisting only of copies of the *Rubaiyat*. At the start of the twentieth century, Sotheran's (suffering from an unusual and characteristically transitory surplus of cash) took it upon themselves to commission a particularly decadent copy of the book from the talented bookbinders Sangorski and Sutcliffe, who had

---

[*] It used to be a running joke within the company, particularly with those who did the bookkeeping, that Sotheran's has been 'one year away from closing since 1761'.

made a name for themselves with their resurrection of jewel-encrusted bookbinding. Supposedly, Sotheran's told the binders that the cost was to be 'no object', and so it was that the most expensive book ever created came into being. In a misunderstanding largely founded in Sangorski's ignorance of folklore, the binders decorated the covers on both sides with a lavish peacock design, conventionally considered bad luck due to its abundance of 'evil eyes'.

Sotheran's, afflicted by hubris, found the book impossible to sell. So much so, in fact, that in 1911 the book was shipped to New York, where the hope was that it would find a buyer at a newer, much lower price. Alas, when the book reached New York customs they levied a fee which Sotheran's refused to pay (having spent all their money on a jewel-encrusted book). Thus, it made a return trip across the ocean all the way back to London, where it was put into an auction and sold for a miserable price . . . to an American by the name of Gabriel Wells. This time the book missed its intended ship, and was instead safely entrusted to a luxury ocean liner making its maiden voyage, the *Titanic*. It remains at the bottom of the ocean. In a further fit of disaster, the visionary bookbinder Sangorksi drowned several weeks after the book did. In the absence of his partner, Sutcliffe attempted to recreate the book, which was stored in a secure bank vault and bombed to smithereens during a German air raid.

The point of this story is that the only people who say it's not possible for a book to be cursed are people who haven't stumbled across one yet.

The Sotheran tradition of selling cursed books remains

strong to this day. Recently, for example, in one of his non-gourd-related spending fits, Andrew acquired a stunning book which fell into the category of Fine Bindings, leather-clad bricks where the value of the book largely resides in the skill of the bookbinder. With its lavish fine binding dripping with unnecessary gold ornaments, the copy of *Fanny Hill* was a decadent piece which demanded attention. As I am sure you can imagine, it became an albatross around our neck. Andrew spent more time than I am sure he would have liked trying to find someone to take it, and its continued presence on the shelves began to feel like a bad luck charm.

The book stood out at a distance. You couldn't put it on the shelves with the general literature because it turned any dignified display of books into a carnival attraction. If you placed it on its own, then it drew curious passers-by like moths to a flame, which was unfortunate because at a glance the illustrations gave a very good idea of what the story was about. I doubt most of the people who picked up *Fanny* knew what they were in for, and some of them learned a few new things into the bargain before blushing and putting it back where they found it. Someone would ask to look at it several times a week, which meant standing there in discomfort as the unfortunate stranger had an unasked-for encounter with eighteenth-century English sensuality. The wretched book was included in every catalogue, which only made us look as desperate as we were beginning to feel. A year after we bought it, a wealthy Smaug ordered it with a stack of other fine literature, only to return it, on account of how uncomfortable it made him. He's dead now. Later, a second client placed an order, and then vanished into thin air before it could be sent, never to be heard from again. A third client ordered it, only to return it with damage to the spine that he (of course) denied any knowledge of.

As a bookseller, you grow used to encountering cursed tomes every now and then. The regrettable part is that no one you inform about this will hold your claim credible, and it's very difficult to explain to your Accounts department, or the board of directors in their annual review, that a certain portion of the stock isn't really saleable because it keeps killing the customers who try to buy it.

In this storm of cursed books, cryptids and vanishing rubbish bins, months flew by in a blur. With barely enough time to pick up a paycheque, my days were a confusion of unfamiliar people, noises in the dark and afternoons spent frantically perusing dictionaries of antiquarian book terminology trying to find a nice way to say 'a dog has clearly chewed on this copy of *Wuthering Heights*'. Still, the only way out of this situation was through, and I thought to myself that despite everything at least the bookshop itself was something firm to hold on to. A comforting thought, it was, that even if my situation was dire the four walls were not about to come crashing down on my head.

As usual, alas, I was wrong.

Robust lectern, prominently sculpted with ceremonial eagle, likely for religious or ritual purposes. (Additional postage fees required.)

ART
& ARCHITECTURE

A manifest of local features, including but not limited to Sackville Street, the shop configuration and its most conspicuous features &c.

I⊤'s AN OLD bookshop in an old building, and as you can imagine there's a lot of dodgy architectural choices buried under all those bookcases. The Art and Architecture department was discontinued years ago, but the slow process of filtering out the books never really seems to finish. There's a lot to be said about the way the shell of a bookshop influences the people and things inside it, and vice versa.

19

On the Shedding of Skin

IF I HAVE given you the impression that Sotheran's is a place which never changes, frozen in time, then I have misled you. It's comforting to think of a bookshop that way, totally unruffled by the passing of years, a strange sort of anchor for the past. In truth, however, bookshops that refuse to change at all routinely collapse and vanish into the torrent of history. Bookshops have a reputation for being fiscally unreliable, often pulled under the waves of financial ruination in less than a century. It's factually correct to say that Sotheran's, having hung on since 1761, is one of the oldest bookshops in the world, but it's also not true in a lot of ways, because Sotheran's isn't the same as it was when it opened. All the Sotherans are dead, for starters, a long time ago. The bookshop was opened in York, and ended up in London. It moved several times, hopping about like a demented bibliotoad, before finally ending up in Sackville Street, with all the pomp and circumstance of a deflating balloon. What I mean to say is that, despite appearances, Sotheran's has never really been a stranger to change. Even while in Sackville Street, we've only owned certain floors of the property half as often as we might like, and less than twice as much as we deserve.

It should not really have come as a total surprise to the inhabitants, then, when the time came for the Great Upheaval. A passing acquaintance with the Great Upheaval is critical to understanding what Sotheran's is like today. If you're familiar with caterpillar biology, you'll know that in order to emerge as a butterfly, the poor creature has to shut itself away, liquefy and then reconstitute itself. So it was with us. I think it was all the more surprising to the denizens because Sotheran's had been enjoying an uninterrupted period of relative peace and prosperity for decades. Insofar as the shop regulars were concerned, as far as anyone could remember, Sotheran's had always been on Sackville Street, the interior had always spread across a cavernous ground floor, and memories had begun to fade of the ill-fated mezzanine experiment.

The trouble can really be traced back to Sackville Street in the 1930s. Instead of finding a property which they could purchase at a reasonable price like many of their more savvy competitors, the well-meaning manager at the time, a Mr Stonehouse, decided to rent the premises at 2–5 Sackville Street. *After all*, he must have thought, *we can think about buying the shop later.* The spectre of this decision came back to haunt the shop in the twenty-first century, when property even on a cursed thoroughfare like Sackville Street comes at a premium. As a result, the landlords (eager to draw as much blood from the stone as they could) decided to raise the rent on the bookshop accordingly. You could almost hear the vultures circling overhead.

People always complain about their rent, so you might make the mistake of thinking this conventional griping, but bookshops are caught in a uniquely lamentable position. Bookshops require a lot of floor space, an indecent amount of square footage, to function in comparison to many other kinds of retail. Couple that with their notoriously low revenue, and you have a recipe for a Business on the Edge of a Nervous Breakdown.

We don't talk much about the Powers That Be, the owners of the shop who act as directors and benefactors and who sometimes give the shop a pointed kick in the right direction if it needs it. After Henry Sotheran died in his accident, which I think we can all agree was rather thoughtless of him, the company was picked up by a wealthy bookseller and collector turned philanthropist who had resolved that the world needed a place like Sotheran's.* It's been passed from hand to hand ever since, always remaining in the tender embrace of a book lover who wants to support it, eventually landing in the possession of the current owners, who have determinedly sheltered it from the caprice of changing markets for decades. We don't see much of them in person because they practise the retiring kind of benevolent distance which one might expect from philanthropist book lovers.

Despite being busy with other larger and more influential concerns, the Powers make it their business occasionally

---

* The story of Gabriel Wells could fill a book in its own right, but he remains one of the great bibliographic figures to be caught in the Sotheran web. In 1928, it was Wells who saved Sotheran's from near-bankruptcy by purchasing the business, which was a bit like buying a black hole, and he never recovered from the decision.

to check in on Sotheran's. I think perhaps that in the wider, noisy world of commerce it's nice to stop by a bookshop and drink in the quiet. In modern times, it should come as a surprise to no one that the price of renting a shopfront in central London increased year on year, and there came a day when the Powers decided that Something Must Be Done. Work needed doing on several rather important parts of the building, such as the walls, floors and ceilings. A plan was drawn up for the improvement of the layout, partitioning off part of the shop that we could let out to another small business to help with our rent.

About a year after the first tremors of the Great Upheaval were felt on the horizon, the dingy, dusty shop I knew had become a warzone. Walls were caved in. Bookshelves were moved in and out. Boxes of books went in circles around London, flocking like birds without a roost. The entire upper floor was taken apart and reinstalled, reducing it in size so we could rent out some of the space. The Catalogue Room (my favourite room, that tiny secluded heaven away from the outside world) was ripped out and replaced by a gallery space, which came as a great loss to me. In places, however, the shop fought back; the gigantic, hideous metal safes on the ground floor proved impossible to move, and remain an amusing blight on the face of the gallery room.

When the dust settled, we were not the same. Still Sotheran's, but different. Smaller in some places, larger in others. Somehow, we have managed to hold on to the haunted cases which don't close properly, and all of the crooked furniture has slowly but surely insinuated itself back into the shop.

20

The Next Best Desk

WITH CHANGE COMES opportunity. The slow rearrangement of the bookshop, shelves creaking and groaning at all hours as if in protest at the imposition, unveiled a number of peculiar furnishings. A ceramic keg shaped like a beehive emerged out of the cellars, dripping something that smelled like despair. It was placed above several shelves until the veiled remarks from nearby staff (and the inquisitive remarks from customers) caused it to be shoved under a table. Two iron chests emerged from the back, one of which was immediately requisitioned for use as a stationery box.* The crown jewel of this trove, however, was a large writing desk with an expansive surface. The kind of desk a man in my position (still bestride a desk which would have been better appointed as a footstool) might covet. It made my current desk look like a paperweight. As the new layout of the shop began to crystallize, I began to angle for acquisition of the desk, seeing it as a form of karmic justice for my time shackled to Satan's smallest escritoire. To my surprise, the request was granted immediately by Andrew (who in the wake of the renovations was spending more time than usual gazing wistfully into the distance) and he greenlit my carefully rehearsed supplication with barely a

---

* The other remains unopened to this day. When you shake it, something rattles about inside.

second glance. The spacious desk was installed near the door, and in an uncharacteristic fit of vindictiveness I made sure that the tiny desk vanished, never again to torture another innocent.

With glee, I acquired a larger screen, and allowed myself to spread out my spoils. If you stay in bookselling long enough, you acquire a set of reference books specific to your interests (usually 'borrowed' from libraries and other dealers) which decorate your desk area. With a larger desk, I finally had space for Curry's *Science Fiction and Fantasy Authors*, a nook in which to place Gaskell's *New Introduction to Bibliography*, and lots of desk drawers perfect for hiding things that I didn't want to think about.

So there I was luxuriating at my new desk, feet up and basking in the warmth of victory, idly leafing through the pages of a rather valuable eighteenth-century almanac, when the doors opened behind me. I ignored it, naturally. Those heraldic devices weren't going to count themselves, after all, and whoever it was could surely wait until I had finished fully appreciating the scope of my new domain. I have already mentioned that the forces which hold the fate of the bookshop in their hands rarely pay us a visit in person – they are very busy people – and I think it's possible I had grown somewhat complacent. One polite cough later and I was startled out of my seat into an embarrassed kerfuffle as I attempted to straighten myself up.

Whereas booksellers are largely unconcerned with the opinions of passers-by, the smallest comments by the Powers That Be naturally exert substantial influence. A chance remark about the nature of my expansive desk (too large, facing the wrong way, how *interesting*) I overheard with a shiver, like someone walking over my grave.

I came into the shop the next day to find that my wonderful, spacious desk was to be removed. Not only removed, it turned out, but destroyed. Andrew was apologetic in the offhand manner you might adopt if (for instance) you forgot to hold the door open for someone, but not in the way you'd expect someone to be if they'd just given the order to saw apart your dreams. I was bid to remove my things from it, so that the desk could be taken away and reduced to dust before the Powers That Be returned. Solemnly, and with some resentment, I collected my books and piled them in a corner of the floor for want of anywhere else to put them – a tiny shrine to memorialize my eviction. The desk, far too large to be dispatched without a struggle, was dragged away squeaking and groaning.*

Reader, I did not weep. I could only watch as the desk was deposited where workmen still laboured on a distant part of the shop, and avert my gaze as the sound of sawing began. All agreed it was a dreadful shame that such a fine desk had to be cut up into firewood, but what would we *do* with it, was the refrain. We simply don't have a *use* for it, do we.

It took a little while before the penny dropped that if the big desk was destroyed I would need somewhere to put my things. A survey of the cellars was launched, and an

---

* As a rule I do my very best not to hold grudges, but I nurse a few special exceptions.

antique washtable was located which might fit me under it if the legs were raised by perching them on buckets. It was smaller than the original desk had been, and I was moved into a corner behind the doors. I had ended up in a worse situation than I'd been in at the start, and it took a lot of willpower not to hand in my resignation on the spot and turn my efforts to a more rewarding career, like being a crash test dummy.*

At the time I was rather too consumed by the tragedy of my desk to pay much attention to the movements of my colleagues, but the changes to the shop were not only wrought in stone and plaster. In the wake of these events, Andrew disappeared in a puff of smoke to a bookshop up the road, where I hear he is flourishing rather nicely and doesn't have to listen to anyone talk about spreadsheets. I couldn't (and would not) speculate on his reasons beyond the fact that anyone with the courage to oversee the refurbishment of a bookshop like Sotheran's has obviously earned himself a quieter life, but I was grateful to him for taking a chance on me, and I was sad to see him go.

With his departure, it was necessary for the shop to find a new manager. Andrew was replaced by Chris, who was elevated from the Natural History department to govern the rise of Sotheran's from the ashes.

---

* Why didn't I? I suppose I'd become comfortable, that dangerous quality which smooths away all kinds of disappointments.

21

Archives and Arson

THE SOTHERAN'S WEBSITE, until very recently, was a magnificent testament to early computing, and almost entirely non-functional. When you operated it, you could almost hear the clickety clack of Babbage's ghost in the back of your mind. The process for buying a book was so byzantine that it was functionally impossible to order anything at all without waiting several days for someone to remember to check the website for orders and (if they were feeling generous) respond. The website actively interfered with the ability of the shop to take money from customers, to the point where the number of web sales each year was lucky to reach double figures. To my mind, that anyone managed successfully to navigate it at all proved that we had some determined and single-minded customers out there.

The pedestrian performance of the nigh-unusable website was taken as proof by Sotheran's that the internet was clearly a poor way of selling books, and thus it would be foolish to invest in a better website. This self-fulfilling prophecy happily sustained itself for over twenty years, while the website remained out of sight and mind.*

A large part of the old website was dedicated to reminding people how old Henry Sotheran Ltd truly is. The year

---

* This made James very happy indeed, as his relationship with computers was best described as a cold war.

1761 is a long way back for bookshops, which are notorious for being run into the ground by booksellers in the grip of debts, scriveners plagued by addictions, or owners who mysteriously vanished without a trace. The site described Sotheran's as The Oldest Bookshop In The World, which was almost (but not quite) the truth. When it came to making Sotheran's look prestigious and ancient, James was a wellspring of creative ideas and fascinating recollections to which he was the only witness. He had a litany of things he was convinced were true about Sotheran's which he repeated so often and with such earnest conviction that eventually everyone else started internalizing them without ever really bothering to look into them. Was Sotheran's mentioned in a passage by Evelyn Waugh? Yes, he assured us. Or was it Wodehouse? It changed with the wind. Did Sotheran's have a Royal Warrant? Yes, most assuredly. But it was lost. Expired. Destroyed in an accident. Historical evidence was like vintage wine to James, in that he theoretically kept it in reserve for a special occasion but no event ever seemed quite special enough to warrant deploying it. The Oldest Bookshop In The World motif was about as blatant as anything he ever insisted upon – not least because we received periodic veiled threats from a bookshop in Peru which laid claim to the title and seemed to take our assertion as a personal insult. Regardless of the specifics, Sotheran's is veiled in the kind of mystique and legend that can only be found orbiting an institution with genuinely rich heritage. As such, the website waxed lyrical about Sotheran history in a way that was exceedingly enticing to a certain kind of person.

No small wonder, then, that we attracted researchers like flies to a scholarly dungheap. Many antiquarian book-sellers have a deep-seated fear of well-meaning academics. University types with lots of qualifications embody the kind of thorough, diligent curiosity that a bookseller wants to keep miles away from his stock, his business and, in certain cases, his accounting. Perhaps due to James's impressive stream of confident bardic flourishes, or maybe the fact that Sotheran's labels and catalogues are found scattered across the whole of Britain, industrious scholars are con-stantly finding their way to our door with burning questions. Emails with the subject heading 'A request', nervous phone calls and even sternly headed letters cross our threshold almost every day, each asking (in more or less polite tones) to know the answer to some titbit of Sotheran's lore on which hinges the fate of twenty years of painstaking work. 'Have you a copy of the 1871 Sotheran's catalogue on Birds of Paradise?' they say, or 'I'm investigating the life of Horace Moneybother, I do believe he was a client of yours back in 1901, do you have his purchase records?' When col-leges and universities are in term time, requests can come faster and more frequently than genuine book orders or actual clients, and it would take several full-time posts to diligently research and answer them properly. As the lowly apprentice, there was a time when I attempted to engage with these requests, until I started to comprehend that the emails were being passed down to me not because anyone really expected me to deal with them, but because giving them to me meant they weren't on anyone else's desk. The important thing, I eventually ascertained, was that the task had been delegated, and with any luck that would be the last anyone had to think about it. I will never forget Andrew's face as I tried to apologetically explain why I couldn't fulfil a particular research request he'd himself passed down to me several days earlier. He looked completely mystified, as if he couldn't begin to fathom why, just because he had given me a task, I had set myself on such a noble, self-sacrificing and destructive course of enquiry as to complete it.

Inevitably, when we make the mistake of engaging with one of these requests, we don't have the answer they are looking for. The question usually involves some particular lost to the mists of time, or some forgotten treasure last seen in the hands of a Sotheran's employee decades ago. The back and forth can last several weeks. With each volley the intensity of the researcher grows closer to fever pitch until finally they level the question they've been wanting to ask the entire time but hadn't quite worked up the nerve: Can We See Your Archive? The question is put with a strange mixture of rising hope, suppressed fear and quiet satisfaction, as if this is a checkmate from which there is no escape.*

It's a poorly kept secret at Sotheran's that the archives were lost. I don't mean 'lost' in the way that you might misplace your phone, or lose your purse. I mean lost in the

---

* I think, to academics and researchers of the calibre who would go so far as to track down Sotheran's, the thought that an organization as venerable as ours might not possess a well-organized and thoroughly inventoried archive is unthinkable. I find their optimism refreshing.

same way as Atlantis, or the Gardens of Babylon. James would maintain adamantly that the records were 'destroyed in the war'.

The issue became a fairly moot point, however, due to events leading up to Sotheran's 250th anniversary. For the occasion, and perhaps because everyone was sick to death of arguing over it, Andrew enlisted the historical services of a very determined scholar called Victor Gray, who charged himself with writing a company history. In pursuit of this goal, he put together a much smaller archive of all the scrap papers he could find relating to the shop. He delved near and far into libraries and local authority archives across the country to find any remaining trace of the company's past, neatly filing it all into boxes and labelling it with touching diligence. Before he left, he put together a little catalogue detailing the order of this new, pristine archive. And then, his labours expended, he made his way home, no doubt congratulating himself on a job well done.

Reader, we lost the second archive.

It's unclear precisely when it happened. All I know is that I discovered the directory for it some years later in a dark cupboard while I was looking for a tiny printing press I'd squirrelled away in a box in the same environs. Out of curiosity (and because as the apprentice I was being inundated with research requests I had not the means to satisfy), I asked the manager where this new archive was located, and it turned out no one knew. A vague suspicion remains that perhaps it ended up in a storage cellar in Birmingham, but as we've never had any shop outlets in Birmingham and no member of staff lives there, it's genuinely hard to say why anyone would have gone out of their way to do that.

22

Preventative Measures

THE SUITED GENTLEMEN have appeared in the shop without entering through the front door. They slither up the stairs, strumming their suspenders with malicious intent. There are three of them this time, more than usual, but they are as impeccably polished as always. They hover near the political books and then one of them splits off, like the head of a hydra, to ask me as they always do if I have any Ayn Rand. I lead them to the right case and point out some options while they shuffle and sway, trees caught in a stiff wind. They each take a turn to hold the book in their hands, and flash me bright rows of overly white teeth. 'Delightful,' they say, one after the other. 'Simply delightful.' Then they ask a question they've never asked before. 'What if time damages it?' they say. It must be pristine. They must know how we keep our books in such a condition.

We get a lot of questions from people who are just starting out on their book collecting journey about how to look after their books. Most have just spent more money than they ever thought they could on a book, and you can see the question bubbling to the surface of their minds. How to stay the passage of time, how to slow the inevitable atrophy? They think we know something they don't, some secret trick of the trade that ensures a book's immortality. It would be impolite to disillusion them so early on the path of hoarding, so we usually end up talking about light – for aversion to light is what unites both Smaugs and Draculas.

From inside the shop, behind the looming shelves that take up most of the window space, it has always been difficult to tell what kind of day it is outside. Even after the Great Upheaval, we kept a few tall shelves in the main window, blocking out as much natural light as possible from certain angles. On particularly bright days, when the smog relents and the sun beams down cruelly overhead, you'll often find a Sotheran's employee on the street outside the shop holding a ten-foot pole and mired (as far as anyone can tell) in ritual combat with the side of a building. The tussle looks one-sided from a distance, the unlucky jouster repeatedly stabbing the wall above the shop window with a hook on the end of a pole. It's hard to miss, because the intricate dance blocks off that entire side of the pavement, forcing pedestrians to head round the other side, usually muttering darkly to themselves.

This task, one which James seemed to enjoy far more than anyone else, is a custom based primarily on fear of the light. He would peer out of the window each day as the sun rose in the sky, waiting for the first treacherous glare to fall on the window display. With a sudden show of agility, he would skip to a dark corner of the shop and return with one of several hooked poles, taking it out on to the street.

The awnings at the front of the shop are cleverly

designed, in a Daedalian sense, folding nigh invisibly into the brickwork when they aren't in use. Clearly the original architect thought there was some merit in this approach, some unknown advantage in having a hidden marquee stashed in the wall and only reachable with a very unusual tool. It can only be operated by gently manoeuvring the hook into a tiny hole, and then delicately but firmly reversing into the street (risking being hit by one of the infrequent cars which prowl through Sackville Street) to pull the device out, unfurling it into a great awning that blocks the light from hitting the books.

Unfortunately, the designer of this ingenious device failed to account for several things. Firstly, it's actually quite hard to complete this procedure without impaling a passerby on one or both ends of the pole. Secondly, when fully extended, the supports that keep the awning in place are at a level which will clothesline anyone taller than six feet, sometimes resulting in a pile of tall pedestrians with mild concussion.*

When I began my journey as an apprentice, the awning had several unsightly holes, which made it ineffective for protecting against the rain. It was replaced by a new one during the Upheaval, but it became apparent why this was a bad idea soon afterwards. People began to congregate under it in bad weather to have loud phone conversations. I have long since internalized this as a lesson never to fix anything.

---

* This would, I suppose, make them more suggestive customers.

Operation of the awning wasn't solely to gratify James's love of deploying Sotheran's arcana (though that was undoubtedly part of it). Rare books, like people, are almost always made of fragile organic material. If you go out in the sun for hours without a break, you'll get sunburned. If you leave a book unprotected from the glare, it begins to deteriorate. The old shop layout, for instance, included two large skylights at the back, intended to provide natural illumination to the far reaches of the main floor. From the moment I joined, those windows had been covered up with patchwork brown paper by James, who knew that a skylight in an old bookshop was tantamount to slow arson. The front windows to the shop are now fitted with a film to block radiation, and the cases are arranged so that as many of them as possible are out of direct sunlight during the day. Some books are more vulnerable to this than others, but the main culprits are:

1. *Red/Purple.* The two forbidden colours, because so much as a ray of light falling on them causes the dye to fade into an ugly pink or brown. Purple is so notorious for warping to brown that it is something of a running joke. Sometimes, if you're not careful, you find yourself cataloguing a book simply as brown without realizing that it was originally purple – the colour change can be quite convincing.

2. *Vellum.* Conventionally made from calfskin, and with a highly distinctive waxy white finish, vellum is an expensive way to bind a book. It's all the more sad, then, that it is also highly sensitive to changes

in temperature. Leaving a vellum book in the light is asking for it to curl up like a dead spider, and once it's gone there's no way of convincing it to return to its old shape short of shoving it in a vice for a few months and hoping for a miracle.*

If you can keep your books out of the light, then you've won half the battle, but it's not actually that satisfying to have your beloved books locked in a dark box in a cellar where you can never look at them. People inevitably end up putting them on display, tempted by the dark siren song in their hearts, and a few more rare books get added to the pyre.

At this point in my heliophobic diatribe, the Suited Gentlemen stop me with the imperious wave of a hand. They briefly confer among themselves, and then return. It cannot be this simple, they insist. I must have a secret I can bestow for the preservation of books. Tell us, they chorus. Reluctantly, and feeling under pressure, I cautiously admit that Book Oil is always a possibility.

We call it Book Oil because the true list of ingredients was jealously guarded by the supplier, one of those sphinx-like beings for whom we retained only a phone number and a set of initials in a raggedy phone book Andrew kept under

---

* James insisted on keeping all his vellum materials in a hidden cupboard in the cellars, at the back of the staff kitchen. At intervals he would descend to check on them, as if he expected they might have begun to duplicate in the cold, dark conditions.

a pile of random papers on his desk.* The Book Oil arrived at the shop in a series of unmarked bottles made of thick brown glass, to which labels would be assiduously fixed declaring it to be Book Oil, along with a best guess of the active components. It had the air of a Victorian tincture, which would have satisfied the original Sotherans very much indeed, I think. A single whiff of it was powerful enough to knock out a horse, and give everyone who walked into the shop a contact high for the rest of the afternoon.

The oil was for treating leather, in theory. James, who held the only working knowledge of its safe and effective use, would advise that a small dab should be deployed, ideally on a cloth scrap or rag for which the oiler had no further use. Correct application would give new life to a fading leather bookbinding, like the fountain of youth. 'Less is more,' he would say, in the tone of a threat. If one used too little, then you exposed yourself to lethal and unregulated gases for nothing. If you used too much, you'd drown the book in something sticky that would take years to dry out. Frankly, even if you got it right, you'd end up leaving all your books out to quietly digest the oil for a day or two before they could be reshelved, and there was no guarantee that the oil wouldn't do something completely strange to them in the process, a turn of events for which Sotheran's did not offer a refund.

---

* The phone book once came briefly into my possession, but all I was really able to gather from it was that we really don't keep enough information on our contacts.

We sold our last bottle of Book Oil years ago, after the local postman happened to mention in one of his nightly visits that it was in fact illegal to send anything through the post that might spontaneously explode. After some fervent conversation, the last few bottles were flogged in store and no further shipments were ordered. Interestingly, we continue to receive calls from frustrated customers asking after the oil, many of whom seem oddly invested for a conversation about conservation. We do offer a replacement (procured from a more reputable source) which is more of a wax, which doesn't produce quite the same heady effect when opened, and which for some reason hasn't fostered quite the same level of dependence in our clients.

If both of the above measures of preservation prove wanting, then there is another recourse. In the gallery room are the aforementioned two gigantic metal safes, installed when the building was built and sealed into the brickwork in such a way that the builders who were asked to remove them fell about laughing. Both safes are the type with huge tumblers and intricate locks, the kind of safe that one is actually recommended to use in the days of cyber criminality, because no one really trains in how to break them open any more. It's almost a shame that no one knows how to crack them, because one of them has refused to open since 2018, and I dread the day when we actually need to retrieve something from it. When we need to store a delicate book far away from anything that might aggravate it, it goes down into the dark to spend its days in a metal prison with its associates. It's not a remedy for old age, but it's better than any of the alternatives.

When I tell people this, they ask if they should take similar precautions, to which I respond with a question of my own. Why are they buying it? If the answer has anything to do with enjoying it, then no, I don't recommend they stick it in a lightless cell never to be opened again, because books are a form of art, and art was made to be perceived. There is no way to stop the passage of time, and there is no way to prevent a book eventually going the way of all flesh. If you lock it away, and no one ever spends any time appreciating it, it's still going to turn to dust like the rest of us. We do what we do at the bookshop to make sure it survives until it gets to its next owner. All anyone can do is take reasonable precautions. Keep the books away from fire. Don't throw them in a puddle. And remember to take delight in them.

23

Neighbours

THERE'S SOMETHING PROFOUNDLY otherworldly about Sackville Street. Not in the manner of mischievous sprites or sparkly unicorns, but evocative of a strange cairn deep in the country that you warn children away from, or an heirloom necklace made entirely from teeth.

Henry Sotheran Ltd moved into their premises at 2–5 Sackville Street in the 1930s, fleeing a building which was about to be demolished due to decrepitude. The new development, a grand affair built in the Georgian style called Sackville House, was advertised as the first foray into a stunning renovation of Sackville Street, and Sotheran's was delighted to become the first tenant. A bold move, for it involved carting all the books (and bookcases) from the old shop in Piccadilly into the quieter side street, where the shop remains to this day. It transpired, of course, that the rest of the street never received the upgrade it was promised, leaving Sotheran's stranded alone in a street that time forgot. Sackville Street has presided over the downfall of many fledgling businesses, like the ill-fated restaurant Sackville's which opened and closed in the space of a month. A blink of an eye from our perspective, as you can imagine, and a shame given how expensive it must have been to monogram all those plates.

It can be hard to keep track of our neighbours: all around us, people and businesses are constantly moving in and out. Like most London side streets, the buildings here are a strange mishmash of architectural styles, and it's not unheard of for some avant-garde art installation to spring like a poorly conceived Athena from the mind of a budding entrepreneur. A few years ago, for instance, someone decided to erect a huge set of cardboard legs and stick them out of the windows of a house into the street. Some bold artistic point was undoubtedly being made about the nature of legs (or perhaps the nature of houses), but no amount of staring at it allowed the observer to determine exactly what was going on. As time went by and London's semi-perpetual drizzle began to take its toll, the legs slowly warped and became a bow-legged, monstrous horror crouching over the abandoned bike racks. The installation was eventually taken down by a tired-looking man in white overalls, who seems to appear whenever an immersive art piece dies in order to remove the corpse.

Our second closest neighbours inhabit a set of offices above us in what was once the mezzanine floor of Sotheran's. The shop abandoned that floor decades ago, and various companies have moved in since. We don't see much of them apart from on the odd occasion when we accidentally set off the fire alarms for the entire building by opening too many dusty books all at once (which is all the time). And because the building is old – and a bit strange – we have a fire escape tunnel that leads directly into their offices, so (should the need arise) we could at any moment emerge into their offices from below, like a kraken rising from the deep. I'm not sure they are aware of this, so I'm waiting for the perfect moment to spring it on them.

If one dares to head out of the building into the street there's a newsagent which neither time, escalating rent nor rising damp seems able to dislodge. The staff rotate every year or two in response to some unknown environmental factor, presumably a bit like salmon migrating. Each time new staff arrive, they contrive some well-intentioned but ultimately ill-fated gift in an attempt to bond with us. The most recent bunch have decided that we need empty boxes, and frequently bring us whole stacks of them, dumping mounds of cardboard in the foyer like a cat dragging dead bats into the house as gifts. We don't know how they arrived at this conclusion, and no amount of earnest explanation has managed to dissuade them from this course of action, so we did the only polite thing and resolved to drown in boxes.

On the other side, there's a shop called Meyer and Mortimer which sounds like an undertaker but it turns out is actually rather well known in the world of tailoring and shiny buttons. I never see anyone go in, and I never see anyone leave. I tried to deliver a parcel there once; I didn't get past the saturnine doorkeeper, who wielded a pair of fabric scissors with the grim authenticity of a headsman. Rare bookshops and tailors share a strange symbiosis, and if you look carefully you'll often find them inhabiting the same commercial ecosystem, but we don't talk much. I suppose they find our elbow patches to be an offence against the natural order, and we find ourselves unable to afford a new suit. Despite this, the people who buy expensive rare books are often the kind of people who buy themselves new three-piece suits, and so the two kinds of shop circle each other in a balanced duality, their fates tied to one another, doomed never to touch.*

If the apocalyptic lack of shopfronts wasn't enough, the real death knell to Sackville Street is the fact that until recently it was impossible to drive to, a casualty of central London's byzantine one-way system. All maps suggest that driving to Sackville Street involves a good thirty minutes of winding lanes and tiny corners. No cab driver, therefore,

---

* As I write this, I discover that Meyer and Mortimer are moving out, which makes me rather sad, but the prospect of a wine bar perhaps replacing them is fortifying. There will be other tailors, I am sure, but that one was ours.

ends up in Sackville Street by accident. A recent grand plan by the local council to 'reinvigorate' the street entailed reversing the direction of traffic. In theory this made Sackville Street easier to reach, but in the year since it happened people just seem to be heading up and down it in whatever direction they like, resulting in a number of road blockages, randomly parked cars, and taxis going in repetitive circles.

Envision, then, the quality of applicant we managed to source in the wake of the Great Upheaval, when we needed to sublet some of the shop space in order to keep up with the escalating cost of rent. During the 'renovations', a subsection of space was partitioned off from the main shop, with the notion that if we could fool some poor soul into parting with a phenomenal amount of money to rent it from us, it would mean the shop could go on operating in something similar to the same way it always had. Feelers were put out to find a tenant with deep pockets and no knowledge of local mythology, eventually coming to rest on the first of many potential victims, a salad eatery called Vital Ingredient. The staff had to spend several months informing clients that part of the shop would become a salad bar, but then the chain got a look at the actual premises and vanished into the night. There followed a sequence of similar disasters with a variety of clothing shops, pop-up wine bars and seasonal haunts, none of whom got further than the threshold before letting off a sad trombone noise and disappearing.

It's very likely that this had something to do with the interior of the sublet. While the shop had been slowly tinkered with and repaired until it looked like a bookshop once more, the area we were trying to rent had been gutted like a fish and left for dead. The cases (and flooring) had been ripped out, the ceiling dangled a number of concerning wires, and it completely lacked internal plumbing. We were offering, essentially, a haunted shack. To complicate matters further, in the months after the space was created Sotheran's employees slowly began to sneak their oddities into the sublet, creating a kingdom of old furniture, rogue antiques, suspicious black bags and a single gigantic Perspex book stand which no one wanted to take responsibility for.

The quest to find a tenant for the sublet occupied many months, and all the while we had a succession of people coming in to smugly ask us 'what was happening with next door' when they knew very well that it was an abandoned horror show. Eventually, as if the Lord himself had taken mercy on us, the space was picked up by a Japanese retro clothing company called The Real McCoys, who excitedly moved in, seeing the state of the place as a challenge rather than a downside. In a superlative sequence of interior decorating stunts, they transformed it (with the help of some old bookcases à la Sotheran's) into something really lovely, and I hear they are doing very well indeed. I think the late Mr Sotheran would be very happy with them, and not just because he'd look great in a leather jacket.

24

Thieves and Thieftaking

THE BEEPING NOISE has been repeating itself for about half an hour before I work up the courage to say anything. It is a muffled kind of shrill tooting from somewhere near the doors, and everyone is ignoring it. Feeling that I might be developing some kind of tinnitus, or maybe just suffering a long overdue breakdown, I quietly pad over to James and ask him whether this is normal. I know it's not normal, but I can't figure out any way to ask that doesn't seem odd, because clearly everyone can hear it. Beyond anything else, it is distressing the Suited Gentlemen, who have been lurking all morning in front of the economics books and are now looking wildly around as if they have been caught perpetrating a crime. Looking up from a stack of yellow papers, James furrows those bushy eyebrows of his and scowls in the direction of the door as if suddenly realizing what it was that had been bothering him. Disengaging from his stacks of papers like a swordsman from melee combat, he backs over to the doors and uncovers a decrepit pair of plastic obelisks, the kind used to detect shoplifting. A swift kick, and the bleeping peters out to a plaintive whine, then stops altogether.

When you walk into any antiquarian bookshop in London, you are likely to notice that many of the cases are covered over with glass and are shut tight against intrusion. This is true of the upper floor at Sotheran's, where all the cases have locks and to access any of the books you theoretically need to get the bookseller to open them up for you. It's a longstanding grievance internally, with some staff thinking that the closed shelves just ward off anyone who might want to look at books, and others retorting, 'Do you *want* this place to devolve into a den of thieves?'

There are lots of reasons why the rare book trade is a singularly poor target for thieves, the primary one being that the industry is so small. If you manage somehow to make off with an exceptionally rare, one-of-a-kind book, you'll get about halfway down the road before every book dealer in a hundred-mile radius is aware of the theft. All it takes is a quick email to the local book association, and further emails are pinging left, right and centre alerting book dealers to the fact that a Very Specific copy of a book is missing. Book dealers don't tend to carry a vast amount of very expensive books, and many have a vested personal financial interest in counting them before they go to sleep. A wary thief would have to sit on a book for quite some time before managing to find anyone to buy it.

It's far more common for career thieves to target libraries and institutions that have such large holdings and overburdened staff that they might not uncover a missing tome for weeks or months, by which time the thief has already made their profit and disappeared into the mist.

Despite all this, bookshops still get more than their fair share of opportunists lurking around trying to snatch up something on which they can make a quick turnover. Behind the tiny desk at the top of the stairs, James had pinned a selection of blurry pictures (taken with the shop's ancient CCTV camera) which were about as useful as a glass hammer. These, he said, were the local book thieves he had caught trying to pilfer things before. I was not to confront them, he specified, but I was to follow them around the shop. He demonstrated for me, and the art of it was clearly to place oneself at all times so one could see what their hands were doing, while appearing on the surface to be fairly innocently occupying oneself with a book-adjacent task.

The main target of this behaviour was the Scarecrow Man, who regularly came into the shop to try his luck, and with whom James had developed something of a personal enmity. His visits were usually pre-empted by the Booksellers Association, who were (and remain) in the habit of wearily notifying booksellers when he is sighted in the area. He would slip into the shop, draped in a long coat, and the game of cat and mouse would begin. If I squinted at the blurry CCTV pictures, they sort of looked like him in the right light, but his main distinguishing feature was his eyes, which were sunken so far back in his head they were always swallowed in shadow. Sometimes he would wear a big hat, or a long scarf, but James had a sixth sense for when the Scarecrow Man stepped over the threshold, on occasion even predicting it in advance – you could tell something was amiss because he would stand with his head tilted as if there was something foul in the air.[*]

---

[*] I am given to understand that Scarecrow Man ended up in jail for some time, but in recent years has been seen prowling the streets again with increasing regularity. At this point he is almost something of a malevolent trade mascot or bad luck spirit, like a grim or a nuckelavee.

With creatures like the Scarecrow Man lurking in every alley, one has to think of security. The cases around the edge of the shop, rescued from previous incarnations of Sotheran's by overzealous interior designers, each have a tiny lock which secures the cases against intrusion. In fact, all the glass cases have locks, most of which are bespoke and were created by companies that no longer exist. When I was taken on a tour of the shop in my first week, I was shown two sets of keys that opened the cases. These sets looked semi-complete, and each one contained some keys that opened some of the cases. Neither keychain was identical, each had about fifty keys, and most of the keys were never used, but no one was brave enough to throw them away (in case they were needed some day). In addition to this, every desk at Sotheran's has a small collection of random keys, which presumably fit boxes, hatches and locks throughout the shop. Some of the keys were labelled, which was actually less helpful than leaving them unmarked. They would carry words like 'Linnaean Case' because the case had once been bought from the Linnaean Society, as if someone could discern the correct case from that information alone. Important keys were sometimes taken off the keychains (where they could be confused with other similar-looking keys) and hidden in completely separate locations by well-meaning members of staff. As a result, opening some of the cases remains impossible to this day, and books are inserted by opening adjacent cases to drop things through a hole in the side, or the back.

I think every bookseller develops their own method of protecting the books, including locked cases, keeping all their important books at home, or never leaving their desk and taking all their meals in sight of their shelves. There was a brief period, before my time, when Sotheran's deployed an electronic tag system supposed to set off an alarm when anyone left the shop carrying a stolen book, but from the box of unused tags I eventually found it's clear that the effort of including one in every single book grew too onerous. I have personally developed a strategy I call Total Confusion, which is to leave all my books all over my desk shuffled into piles of reference books and rely on the fact that (a) the average thief won't be able to tell the difference between an expensive book and garbage, and (b) in a room full of locked cases I like to think most enterprising criminals would assume that I would never be foolish enough to leave expensive things lying about in an unlocked drawer. Even after all this time, I still can't tell the approximate value of an unfamiliar book on sight, so I defy a random shoplifter to figure it all out in the time it takes to pilfer something from under my nose.

I am fairly convinced that it's for this reason that the books which disappear from the shop seem to be completely random, with no discernible pattern to their price or size. If a book vanishes from a prominent shelf, and no one can offer a reasonable explanation for where it might have gone, we tend to assume it was stolen.*

---

* We are wrong about as often as we are right, with missing books appearing years later in the incorrect department. However, assuming the worst does mean we can stop looking for it, which lets the book find its way back to us in its own time.

25

The Lectern Effect

O F ALL THE EGREGIOUS articles and space-intensive oddities which have been trafficked into Sotheran's over
the years masquerading as stock, it is the lectern which I
think takes the crown of Most Inconvenient. A gothic
wooden affair which rose a foot or two off the ground, it
held just enough space for an energetic preacher to clam-
ber up and make a congregation feel bad about their life
choices. The book rest where the bible would be held (leaving arms free for gesticulation) was carved into the shape of
a huge wooden eagle. I'm given to understand this is the
kind of eloquent and confusing metaphor one expects in a
place of worship, as the talons of the divine descend from
above in a flurry of wings and death, but it seemed to alarm
people to come face to face with the beaked fury of God as
they entered the bookshop.

The lectern arrived as something of a surprise, because
Andrew had purchased it at a European auction some time
earlier and then pushed it to the back of his mind. This was
the kind of purchase that one would try not to inform the
Accounts department about until after it had arrived. The
lectern had seemed like a good idea at the time, or so
Andrew said, but by the time the delivery men had lugged it
across the continent to Sackville Street there was absolutely
no way they were taking it back so the question of whether
or not the purchase was a good idea was immaterial. It was

deposited by the door of the shop, a decision motivated by the fact that it was very heavy.

The lectern proved stubbornly resistant to any attempts to sell it, not only because the price label kept getting lost and no one could see it under the boxes, but also because most customers don't bring a forklift with them to the shop. For a while it caused a nuisance, with regular visitors like the Ancient refusing to change their usual route around the shop and repeatedly walking into it like a lost Roomba rather than going around it, but slowly over a period of several months it began to fall victim to assimilation.

Assimilation begins softly, barely perceptible to the naked eye. You'll be making your way across the shop with a box, minding your own business, when something distracts you and you need to put it down. You're in a hurry, and all the surfaces are full of books. It won't hurt, you suppose, just to place the box down for a few moments on this expensive lectern which is technically for sale. No one will even notice. So you walk off to deal with whoever got their thumb trapped in the book vice today, and when you finally return a few days later there is no lectern for sale at all, only furniture. The entire lectern has been subsumed into the shop.

The shop is a cemetery of objects that shouldn't have become part of the furnishings. We uncovered the bell jar containing Dave during the course of the renovations, behind a faulty carriage clock which James would 'fix' every week using a hammer. The bell jar was so covered in grime that it had faded into the background, but on bringing it down to ground level and giving it a quick wipe, we discovered a stuffed owl hiding inside. I made the mistake of asking Chris to name him, thinking we'd settle on something distinctive like Aloysius, and so Dave the Owl joined the staffing team as unofficial shop mascot.

He'd been installed on some decorative vegetation, which had rotted and withered away into a gnarled sort of bracken. His feathers were a ghostly white, though an ornithological inspection by Chris (our resident expert on all things natural history) revealed that Dave used to be a barn owl, and that his albinism was the result of age. No one knew exactly where Dave had come from, though there was a suggestion that some long-ago director had left him with us for safekeeping. Either way, he is a Sotheran's fixture now, and remains our mascot, even if Chris doesn't like him very much and keeps trying (unsuccessfully) to sell him when no one else is looking. I suppose that one of the burdens of management must be learning to live with macabre artefacts in your vicinity, as long as they boost morale.

As you come into the shop, if you look carefully, you'll see two busts sitting by the door together. One, James always claimed, was of Shakespeare, though it could very easily be any bearded man with a poetic countenance. The other is quite distinguishable as the poet John Milton, identifiable chiefly by his sour expression. These were once intended for sale, though the fact that we can't prove the first one is Shakespeare, and the latter has a distinctly dissatisfied mien, resulted in them surviving long enough to develop their own personalities. At different times of year they get hats, or masks. Sometimes I use Milton as a door-stop, if I feel he's being particularly cantankerous. Mostly I find that I am unwilling to separate them; like two animals who have shared a pen their entire lives, I feel that they might be lonely apart.

I suppose that anything can become part of the shop if left hiding in plain sight for long enough. Behind every cupboard door and on top of every shelf is another relic which was once important to someone, now faded into the background. Perhaps that's part of the fundamental charm of an old bookshop. No curio left behind.

26

Waterworks

I F YOU ARE one of the five or six people who walk down Sackville Street each day, and if you manage to avoid being hit by a confused taxi heading in the wrong direction, or being clotheslined by the Sotheran's awning, you might notice that towards the end of the street the pavement becomes rather strange underfoot. In what could be mistaken for an honest blunder, the flagstones in front of Sotheran's have been replaced with a combination of concrete and thick glass squares. From above, these squares seem grey, thanks to the accumulated grime of many decades, and a passer-by might not give them more than a confused second glance. Some people even take the time to stomp on them.

Deep below the surface of the earth, daylight filters through some of the panels to a hallway which runs under the shop. This unusual and impractical architectural feature is anecdotally attributed to a Mr Knott, an erstwhile employee and cellar worker of Sotheran's who (if legends are true) had his own somewhat lecherous reasons for wanting glass panels overhead. Whether this is true or not, whoever installed the glass was a poor architect, as the course of years caused the glass to quickly acquire a layer of filth that reduced the light to a dim kind of twilight. No ladder is tall enough to reach the panels from below and clean them, which perhaps thankfully means they've been dirty for all of living memory. Looking up at the panels from below gives one the sense of being trapped in an oubliette.

In time, Mr Knott shuffled off the mortal coil, and the original intent of the glass flooring was forgotten. What could not be changed, however, was the fact that glass makes for an exceedingly inadequate construction material for a London thoroughfare, even one as starved of foot traffic as Sackville Street. The steady tramping of feet overhead, coupled with the steady rumble of the underground, began to slowly crack the glass.

In consequence, whenever it rains, water leaks through the cracks and wends downwards into the shop basement. In normal London conditions, when the rain trickles down in intermittent fits and bursts, this manifests as a slight dampness, but in the winter months the various tributaries trickle all the way down to the floor. In the process they almost always manage to find the light switches (placed there by electrical engineers who clearly carried out the job on a bright summer's day) and so the cellars are particularly gloomy even for Sotheran's. When the water reaches the floor, the tributaries join together into a single flow which heads downhill and pools near the staff kitchen.

Two, and only two, prospective 'solutions' to this problem have ever been enacted.

First, a complaint is made to the landlord, which grumbles up through the staff until it reaches some faceless creature in a faraway office block. A complaint made in this manner functions as a sort of invocation, which (after a waiting period somewhere between three days and for ever) summons an extraordinarily unprepared-looking old man carrying a small tube of sealant. He doesn't tell anyone that he's arrived, but one can see him through the window staring at the street and whistling through his teeth in the way tradesmen do when they know they're about to disappoint you. Eventually, when he's exhausted the full length of time someone can stand on a street staring at the floor without looking suspicious, he sighs, and begins to plug up whatever cracks and gaps he can find with silicone. As soon as he has left, the thumping and rumbling of subterranean London begins to dislodge his efforts, and a few days later the tiles are as permeable as ever. In the night hours I am haunted by the possibility that, seeing as no one ever really checked his name or credentials, he might have nothing to do with the landlord at all, and is just a distressed local citizen with too much time and Unibond on his hands.

The other solution? Buckets. James enjoyed hoarding containers, and so it was no surprise to me when he produced a motley array of pails and bowls whenever it started to rain, carefully placing them by memory in areas where he knew water would drip through. Navigating the cellars during rainy season is to hop, skip and jump an obstacle course of half-full buckets.

Considering how much the business depends on keeping stock dry, it actually always seems like things are getting wet in Sotheran's. Several years into my apprenticeship a flat roof located somewhere in the crooked architectural sprawl above the shop began to gather water after stray waste blocked the single, inadequate drainage pipe. The problem went unnoticed at first, with the rising damp causing a nasty smell that no one could triangulate, until one night the water seeped through a back wall, destroying entire shelves of precious books and leaving a fetid puddle on the floor. The bookcases were removed, to reveal a hideous mould infestation spreading across the entire wall. If you looked at it sideways, it resembled a frowning face. Once the mould had been uncovered, the smell increased in intensity until the entire shop reeked of death. It was a pleasant deterrent against casual customers, but rather unpleasant to work near. Another letter was drafted to the landlord, complaining that we couldn't do business in an environment actively hostile to mammals, and so after a considerable wait they provided us with several gigantic dehumidifiers which spent the better part of a year making an awful noise like a rocket taking flight and drove people away about as effectively as the smell.

Troublesome as this was, however, it was an excellent excuse for me to spend some time out of the shop, or so I argued. Not that anyone could hear me over the din, but I presumed they were agreeing, and so the next stage of my education began.

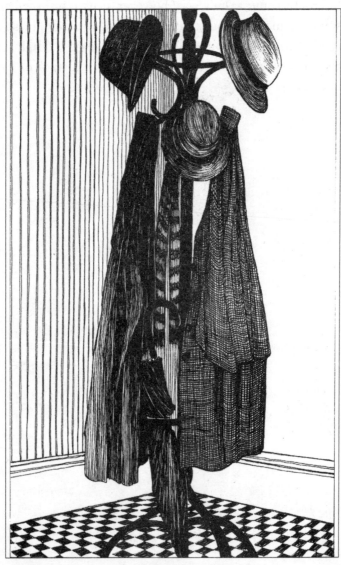

Wooden hatstand, to aid in the facilitation of regulated merriment.
Provenance highly contested.

TRAVEL
& EXPLORATION

*A description of the life of the shop beyond its hallowed walls,
in which our protagonist finds himself in strange and unfamiliar
surroundings, often against his will.*

BOOKSELLING IS NOT a profession in which you are
generally considered to be 'going places', but it is a
profession which requires you to go to lots of places. The
Travel and Exploration department covers anything that
happened in another country, or maybe books that
originated in other countries. Or maybe things in foreign
languages. 'Anything that didn't happen in England' is
really quite a large remit, so it gets an entire wall of the
shop to itself, organized by continent unless Georg is in a
whimsical mood and decides to shuffle things about. If
you want a reminder as to how staggeringly vast the world
is, then the Travel and Exploration department is a good
place to start.

27

Opening Hours

IT'S A BRIGHT morning in London, and I'm wrestling my way through the crowds at the station, trying not to jostle my bag too much in case I damage the book inside. I'm running late, for no good reason whatsoever, and I speed-walk down Piccadilly at the velocity to which a gay man in the capital city is accustomed. I almost get hit by two cars and a horse, and I take a shortcut through one of those construction sites whose tasks never seem to end, saying hello to the regular postman who is arguing with the owner of a nearby shop that sells bizarre rugs and has a scary tiger statue in their window. The life of a bookseller is a relatively mobile one, and even your lowly apprentice finds himself running from place to place handing in fetch quests that wouldn't be out of place in the lower levels of a fantasy video game.

That being the case, making sure that there's always someone on the shop floor during opening hours is a priority, but not one which anyone really wants to be responsible for (the expression 'herding cats' springs to mind). James and I were often in the shop together, because he never seemed to leave, and because as the apprentice I was expected to cover the front desk at all times. On Saturdays, however, we frequently found ourselves alone.

Each Saturday was a chance to learn about something new, objects and books he would hold aside in the week so we could discuss them when we were alone. As we worked, we would talk. I came to understand that he was a private man, so each of the few glimpses he gave me into his life was an act of trust I have no wish to repay with indiscretion. We'd had similar lives in some ways, and it seemed to matter to him a great deal that I didn't enter the world of rare books unprepared for what I might find, enough that he would make the effort of pulling his favourite stool over to my cramped little desk along with a stack of books every week. His wealth of experience never really made it into the shop catalogues – he abhorred a computer – but he carried in that brain of his a lifetime of practical bookselling experience, much of which he left to me piecemeal, without me even comprehending what he was doing at the time.

Opening on Saturdays is a practice we have since largely discontinued.* It was a bone of contention among the staff. No one wanted to work on the weekends, and so a careful rota was negotiated, which I think to this day holds the dubious honour of being the most carefully and consistently maintained piece of paperwork ever to originate in the bowels of Sotheran's. In theory it assigned two booksellers to each Saturday in such a pattern that we would all work the odd weekend with a different member of staff. In

---

* We occasionally do it in December, which enrages and confuses just about everyone.

practice, the rota was massaged to suit individual interests, and to avoid two booksellers who could not stand each other from being trapped together all day.

For instance, Andrew and James had desks crammed cosily into the Literature department, which is a nice way of saying that even during the week they couldn't really avoid each other. On top of this, James's desk was so messy that he couldn't really get to it except to retrieve stashed objects, so he did most of his work on top of a small glass standing case that doubled as an impromptu writing desk. This case adjoined directly to Andrew's desk, so the two booksellers spent the lion's share of every day staring into each other's work area. As a result, they were inside each other's personal space for five days a week, and I'm not sure either of them found the idea of spending a sixth in that way appealing.

The Sotheran's schedule including a Saturday opening was by tradition, but the hours were shorter at either end. The reason for this, as far as I could tell, is that the busiest times of day for a bookshop are often at about 9 a.m. just after opening and at 6 p.m. shortly before closing – shaving a few hours off either end of the working day means that anyone working a Saturday is spared those more crowded moments. I suppose it didn't seem entirely peculiar – many bookshops have unusual opening conventions. A shop down the road from us, for instance, opens only on select days of the week. Another opens only at certain times of day. Some like to mix and match, creating a confusing calendar of half days which, from the outside, seems designed to stop anyone getting inside.

Compared to some of our colleagues in other book-shops, Sotheran's was able to open six days a week, and rather long days at that. You might think that this would make us more accessible, but this was and remains primarily achieved by having someone at the front desk to take messages. Booksellers are out of the premises almost as often as they are in them, hunting books across the country for sale in the shop. Though we do rely on book runners to bring us stock, a bookseller also needs to be comfortable heading out into the wild to search out things for the shelves. With experience comes the urge to spread your wings and discover something exciting, and as I began to shed my apprentice feathers for full-grown ones, I too began to look beyond the nest.

28

Steeplechase

THE LETTER WAS an innocuous one at first glance. At Sotheran's, we receive many just like it every week. Criminally vague, on headed paper stamped with the crest of some long-forgotten lineage, each one begins something to the effect of 'Dear Sirs' and exhorts us to visit their estate to assess the books of a deceased and distant family member who we are assured was in the habit of collecting rare and impressive books. We would answer a number of these queries – those that don't seem like the opening chapter of a Stephen King novel – and toss the rest into a rubbish bin (whereupon, of course, James would recycle them into the shop proper). The letters deemed realistic proposals were usually then delegated to a bookseller who had some vague knowledge of the subject matter, lived near the area, or otherwise drew the short straw. On this occasion, the letter in my hands had gone unclaimed, largely because it was supremely unhelpful, and on any other day it would have ended up being tossed away. I was determined, however, to get some practice under my belt with looking at books off site, and this seemed like as good a place to start as any. A quick phone call to someone who sounded tinny but very reasonable and I'd locked in a date for a house visit, all on my lonesome.

This was an important moment for me, because though I'd often attended smaller collections or visits inside London, this was a chance to get a look at a whole house of books all by myself. There's a certain kudos that comes with discovering a cache of rare books, particularly in the wild, and something in me hungered for one of those moments. A treasure-hunting instinct, perhaps, that more experienced antiquarian booksellers know to treat with caution.

I planned my journey carefully enough. A train to my destination, and then a reasonable walk to the house. It wasn't very well mapped as an area, but it seemed like a straightforward expedition. As a non-driver, it didn't occur to me to take a car or hire a cab, aside from which it was promising to be a sunny day and I'd convinced myself that a brisk walk was just the thing to shake the cobwebs out of my head after a long train ride.

A bright spring morning rolled around, and I set off, the train pulling into the provincial station which was overgrown but not completely abandoned. Spotty internet access on my phone pointed the way, down a dirty little side track which looked more like a fox run than a public footpath.

A short walk to the property, it had been described as. As I ventured further into the greenwood, I became intimately familiar with the depth of that understatement. Stinging nettles crowded the path at regular intervals, which was laced with tricksome side roads and turnabouts. A variety of foxes, feral-looking cats and what may have been a badger bumbled across the path, which slowly disintegrated until it was just me walking through a forest, cursing to myself. Walls of twisted metal grating, surely a lockjaw threat, sometimes blocked the way, forcing me to wend around them through a scarecrow field or a patch of brambles.

As the path phased in and out of reality, and I wrestled with my GPS to get bearings, I began to notice I was not alone. Behind me on the path, almost out of sight, something was following me. For a brief moment I allowed myself to think this must be a local, and that I should ask directions, before the thought was suffocated by a series of more important questions like 'Who lives out here?' and 'Why are they so large?' I picked up the pace, moving at unwise speed through the thorns and leaves, never quite leaving my shadowy companion behind for long. At one point I dared to wait, thinking that perhaps an innocent hiker would overtake me, but none came.

An hour after I'd started walking, the GPS blinked back

to life and directed me to a set of stone steps leading up to train tracks through the woods, over which I raced with only a faint concern for whether or not a train was imminent. On the other side, tripping down the steps, I plunged into a cornfield filled with corvids, which scattered screaming into the air.

Picking up the trail, saved only by the blessing of long legs and a lupine gait, I emerged through a hedge into the garden of a quiet country estate, surrounded by carefully pruned trees and an autumnal air. Walking through piles of fallen leaves, it genuinely seemed as if I'd walked right out of one season and into another. Cars were parked out front, and I staggered over, covered in thorns and generally looking like I'd been dragged bodily through a midden. The gentleman in the foyer had the decency to look shocked. 'Walked?' he said. 'No, no one walks here. No one would have told you to walk here.' I fixed him with an icy expression, and asked to see the books.

She had died a while back, he explained as he led me through the house. A fixation with spiritual matters, apparently, had consumed much of her life. 'Spent a great deal of time praying,' he noted ominously. Her legacy, such as it was, included only her crumbling mansion, some puzzling furniture and an arrangement of old books, most of which were in French (and thus were beyond my power to read). I picked up a volume of gothic poetry mostly out of courtesy, and listened to the inheritors begin to bicker over the furniture. Otherwise the house was incredibly quiet, and the more I looked around the more I began to find that the books were largely decayed almost beyond rescue, leather withered into strips, falling apart under my fingers. Bright morning passed into a grey afternoon as I found literally nothing of note, and the family members littered about the house appeared to ask odd questions. Did I mind if they watched me? Could they persuade me to take a walk outside? Did I have any thoughts on this peculiar lockbox with no key? The more time elapsed, the more the interactions began to feel less innocent and more distinctly predatory, as if some measure of my character were being sought.

In a moment when the house seemed to fall still (clutching the copy of verse like an amulet), I entered the rooms under the kitchen, where the previous occupant had stored yet another cache of books. This collection spanned the wall up to the ceiling, books jammed into a zigzag pattern. No lights in this room, so I turned on my phone's torch, and got a bit closer to the shelf. A brief scan of the titles illuminated a theme – *Saving Yourself Through the Lord* was followed by a book of stories about exorcisms, and a variety of paperbacks for children about divine miracles in the face of demonic power.

Reader, I was up the stairs and heading for the door before the dust could settle in the basement. A dark figure or two materialized to ask if I was finished with my appraisal, and noticing the book of poems in my hands, seemed to find this acceptable. A fine choice, they agreed; should I not be getting home, before it started to get dark outside? The question seemed pointed. Eager to leave the house, I excused myself and dashed back to the station through the thickets and twisting lanes. This time, there was no sign of my shadowy observer, and the journey seemed to be over in a flash, almost as if by taking a book from the house I had provided it with what it wanted, and was released from the nightmare.

I arrived at the shop with a torn shirt (a victim of the brambles) and clutching only a single book for my troubles, which had a faint air of malevolence about it. The general (silent) consensus among the booksellers seemed to be that this was what one had to expect from conducting a house visit, and that if I wanted to avoid ripped shirts, then I should acquire a sturdy jacket.

29

Portraits in the Attic

I LEARNED QUICKLY FROM this experience that one shouldn't stray too far from home when searching for undiscovered wonders.* It seemed appropriate, then, when the next visit assigned to me was a genteel town house in London, the kind of witheringly tall, emaciated dwelling which would once have been considered a modest home for a family of four and is now worth the kind of money people murder each other for. It had a stout wooden door and a knocker in the shape of a screaming demon, rimed in a

---

* If you really must, then remember to bring a torch, a robust jacket, and fifty feet of rope.

verdigris disturbing enough that I resolved to bang on the wood instead of touching it.

I stood on the doorstep for quite a while before anything happened, enjoying a few quiet moments to myself. It was one of those few remaining residential areas in the city where they haven't got round to ripping up the trees, and apart from the ever-present tendrils of low-hanging smog, it seemed like a good omen.

The door yawned open on silent hinges without my noticing, and I turned round to see my host standing there wrapped in a cocoon of shawls, hands on her hips. How long had she been standing there? Why hadn't she said anything? She had a stare that made you want to go home, head to bed early and wake up as a gigantic beetle, never again to be burdened with the responsibilities of polite society.

A long moment passed as she looked me up and down, and her expression turned sour as she clearly was not seeing what she'd expected to see. People have strange ideas about how an antiquarian bookseller should look. I suppose most people never think about it at all, but if they do, then they seem to conceive of a late-middle-aged man in tweed with a twinkle in his eye and a penny farthing waiting to whisk him away to his next adventure. Indeed, when I first turned up to Sotheran's I did so in a suit, before it became apparent that I was only going to ruin it with grime and no one seemed to care whether I turned up in suspenders or a potato sack. By nature, I am what you would probably describe as a boggart, in that I slouch up to wherever I need to be in whatever comes to hand as I crawl out of the book-riddled pit I call a bedroom, and it was to this comfortable way of life that I had returned. If I happen to have a shirt on, it is backwards. The last time I saw a tie, it was being lashed to a dodgy piece of furniture so it could support more books.

Anyway, there I was in my favourite cardigan, which was unravelling slightly at the sleeves in the way I like, a worn-out old satchel slung over my shoulder and glasses mended with tape.* My client's face had reached a level of disapproval I can only assume she usually reserved for violent criminals, clowns and other disturbers of the peace. I introduced myself, and she stepped aside to permit me into her home, keeping a wary distance as if tomfoolery of some description might manifest at any moment.

I might have mentioned the house was tall, but it somehow retained room for a grand entrance, with a red-carpet staircase sweeping up around the side. The bookshelves, embedded into the walls of the room, stretched high up into the floors above, most of them dangerously inaccessible without the benefit of winged boots, or a winch. We should start at the top, she said, striding up the stairs as I hurried in her wake. The staircase evened out eventually on to a landing with a fixed wooden ladder leading up to an attic. Up that ladder, she said, was her husband's studio.

---

* My glasses are always broken. I have come to accept this as a cosmic truth, because there is no other way of explaining how I manage to reliably destroy them within twenty-four hours of acquiring them. No number of spare pairs or emergency replacements has ever managed to forestall this for more than a few days.

Before he died, he'd left some books up there, and I was to look through them. She would not go with me.

Alas, the ladder was poorly designed and missing several rungs, so I only noticed after I'd entered the attic through a hatch that the room was far too small for me. Clearly she had been married to someone very short indeed, because I was forced to creep about hunched. Mercifully, an open window let in light from outside, revealing the true purpose of the attic. Portraits of a wrinkled face were hung from every wall, some in frames strapped to the wall, and others hanging loose from ropes across the ceiling, giving the place a Dorian Gray Photography Darkroom aesthetic. The man depicted in the portraits, who I could only presume was her late husband, was either asleep or dead in every picture, and the desaturated colour choices did not make it easy to rule out the latter. Pictures crowded the area, many of them underfoot, and I spent about five minutes up there trying to get under or around them to find the books before deciding that I was not being paid enough for this, and headed back down to break the bad news. I didn't locate any books, but I wasn't going to admit that in case she insisted I go back up.

The little old lady was not to be deterred. Backing me on to the staircase, she pointed at the incredibly tall bookcases which ran around the inside. 'What about these?' she said, impatiently. As politely as I could, I asked how she thought I could reach them. Perhaps she could supply a ladder? This was met with a cascade of tuttings and harrumphings, and she crashed away into the house proper, clearly expecting doors, furniture and anything as inconsequentially mundane as physical objects to accommodate her passage by moving spontaneously aside. A considerable wait followed, during which I stood on tiptoes and craned my neck to try and get a good look at the titles. I was not overly enthusiastic. Even from my current vantage point, I could see piles of mouldering paperbacks and faded spines, and the occasional leatherbound volume already half consumed by blight. It did not reek of promise so much as mildew.

In time she returned holding a small stepladder. Well, more of a glorified footstool, really.

She looked at me. I looked at her. We both looked at the stepladder.

It eventually took my staging a rather dangerous demonstration live on the stepladder to convince her that adding a few steps to the equation did not solve the core problem of hundreds of books sitting far out of reach. She quite openly seemed to consider this a personal failing of mine, as if my refusal to scale forty feet of bookshelves like a spider monkey was a deliberate attempt to frustrate her efforts. We reached something of an impasse and, with no way to reach any of the books short of demolishing the wall with heavy machinery, we had to move on. Despite my longing glances at the front door, and despite the fact she clearly believed I was not up to the task, she insisted we head down into the basement.

There are not, in my experience, a great many legitimate reasons to lavishly outfit your basement. Stepping down into the dark, and looking around by torchlight, we passed by a large green door studded with nails. It had a huge central keyhole, almost ominously ceremonial. She stopped for a moment, pointed at it, and told me that on no account was I to enter that room. Of course I could not as I did not have the key, but she warned me anyway. Trailing loose threads from her many shawls, we turned a corner into what she described as the 'library'.

I don't know for sure if there's an architectural period in which it was fashionable to cram toilets into tiny basement rooms, but in this instance someone had gone to great effort to make this happen. The wonky commode was balanced precariously on an uneven floor, and the walls of the room were lined with hundreds of books containing *Punch* cartoons.

If you're not familiar with *Punch* cartoons, the only funny thing about them any more is how difficult they are to sell. If you've ever glazed over at a comic strip in the paper because you didn't get the reference, then you already know what to expect when you pick up a vintage *Punch* almanac. Oblique political jokes from a century and more ago, referencing contemporary events no one remembers and people who have been long forgotten, they often turn up in huge, dense albums, and our general feeling in the present day is that no one has the space to store them. I often think their only remaining practical use would be in the construction of pyramids, or hydroelectric dams. Anyway, a bit like one-hundred-volume encyclopaedias, they are very much the last thing you want to stumble across as a bookseller. Trying to convince someone who has been holding on to these things for so long that the cartoons are no longer comprehensible, let alone funny, is the kind of conversation that tends to go downhill very quickly. As I tried to figure out a way to break the bad news to her, I realized she'd left me alone, and in a moment of idle curiosity I pulled the chain to see if the toilet still worked.

I don't think anyone noticed when I arrived back at the shop with wet shoes, and if they did, they had the decency not to mention it. I stashed the ruined shoes under my desk to hide the evidence.*

30

Hatstands and Hauntings

SOTHERAN'S HAS BEEN hijacked for many an unusual event over the years, and if you look closely you can usually find discarded relics from ancient saturnalias embedded in the decor. For instance, a colossal (and lamentably empty) champagne bottle has been wandering about the shop for over a decade. Opinion is divided over whether it constitutes a nebuchadnezzar or a balthazar, but everyone agrees it would be a shame to throw it away, even if it no longer serves any real use. The shop is littered with similar flotsam and jetsam, all of which probably belonged to someone before it became assimilated into the shop.

One cloudy morning rather early in my apprenticeship, Andrew decided to make use of the fact that he now had a

---

* One of those shoes immediately vanished. I do not know where it went.

shiny neophyte to play with, and perhaps drawn by a pang of conscience decided to return an inconveniently sized hatstand to a local bookshop with which Sotheran's maintained a wary truce. This hatstand, I should mention, is passed back and forth to whichever bookshop is having a party in ceremonial fashion, like the Stone of Destiny. A perceptive observer might remark that a hatstand is a relatively easy thing to acquire, and they might wonder why Sotheran's did not purchase their own hatstand. Alas, I wasn't given much opportunity to ponder this, because the artefact was being committed to my custody with a short list of directions and a cheery farewell. It did not disassemble into helpful pieces, neither did it have wheels. I briefly considered hailing down a cab to expedite the process, but it didn't take me long to figure out that any black cab driver worth their salt would divert down a side street at the mere sight of me carrying a gigantic hatstand, and it wouldn't have fitted inside anyway.

It proved to be a bad idea to carry it upright, after I almost knocked the sign off the outside of the shop, and carrying it sideways was asking for trouble. That being the case, I had to wield it like a jousting lance, which was unfortunate for anyone who happened to be standing to the front, back or sides of me. My destination was a bookshop called Jarndyce, in the shadow of the British Museum.*

---

* Named, I have always assumed, after *Jarndyce v. Jarndyce*, the fictional probate case in Dickens's *Bleak House*. For those who don't spend their days immersed in Dickensian arcana, the term is something of a byword for endless legal filibustering.

Specialists in nineteenth-century literature, they've been at 46 Great Russell Street since 1986, though their building has been lurking there since the 1730s. The Jarndyce ghost is supposedly a Scotsman in a kilt, and we have been assured that there is no reason to believe he's malevolent.

In order to get there, I felt I had no choice but to cross into Piccadilly and over the legendary roundabout. If you've never had the misfortune to try and cross Piccadilly Circus on foot, I cannot recommend it. The whole place is a byzantine maze of crossings, poorly placed traffic lights and sudden turns into oncoming traffic. It's also a popular tourist attraction, perhaps due to the immense and highly distracting electronic billboards which flash at road users' eyes. (I have long been of the opinion that the system was designed as a passive-aggressive form of population control.) My flailing attempts to avoid goring an old lady with the prongs only caused me almost to knock another gentleman sprawling, and I was the victim of a gaggle of camera-toting adolescents, who no doubt to this very day hold photographic evidence of my struggles somewhere in their vaults. At this stage in my bookselling development I had yet to shed the masquerade of a suit, and so there I was, tie fluttering into my face, hauling a vast wooden trident across one of the busiest traffic exchanges in the world, accompanied by a swarm of ever more interested tourists like the queen bee of a hive.

I managed to shake them off the trail by darting into the side streets behind Shaftesbury Avenue, where the gay district meets a network of theatre back-door entrances – with stranger things happening in the background, I stopped drawing quite as much attention. A brisk walk and something akin to a pole vault across one more life-threatening road later and I found myself in the right street, a hop, skip and a jump from the British Museum.* The road was noisier than ours, but it's quite difficult for any other road to imitate Sackville Street's seductive torpor.

You can identify almost any London antiquarian bookshop by the style of their signs, without even reading them. They'll usually have a painted wooden board either stuck to the wall or hanging out from a fancy ornate metal arm, and they all seem to use the same font. There's also an absurd number of book dealers who independently decided that green and gold would be their colour scheme, so people often wander into one shop having quite reasonably mistaken it for another completely different enterprise. Jarndyce have spared no expense, and their signs are splashed across the wall, while also jutting out overhead to lure in passers-by. It really is a very attractive shop, though the books stored in the small street-level windows meant I couldn't really see inside. Bedraggled as I was, hope returned to me, and I lugged the wretched hatstand up to the big red door, looking for a way in. It didn't give way to a push, or a nervous shove. I rapped the big metal knocker a few times, to no response. Oh no.

After waiting a while sat on the large stone step in front of the shop, I resolved that I would not be returning to Sotheran's with the stand. For a brief moment of weakness

---

* Or, as I've heard it referred to in these parts, the Evidence Locker.

I considered hiding it in a bush and running for it, but I was a touch afraid that James would sniff out the crime and make me return for it. Eventually, unable to gain anyone's attention, I began to slink off back in the direction I had come from. As I passed the next shop, which appeared to deal in old coins and other collectibles, I poked my head in the door and asked if they knew whether Jarndyce was closed.

The lady behind the counter in the coin shop had a motherly air, or perhaps I projected on to her in my desperation. I barely had time to stutter out my problem before she loudly cursed in a manner of great exasperation and got out a broom. Smiling kindly at me, she told me to follow her, and marched out into the street, trailing me along behind her. I protested that I should maybe leave and come back another day, but she would not hear of it. Rapping on the big red door with her broom, she hollered for someone to 'open up', and arched her neck to look into the windows like a cat peering into a mousehole. I softly began to wish that the earth would swallow me whole, as people wandering down the street watched Coin Lady knock repeatedly on the door of the bookshop like a bailiff, or the angel of death. Vindication of these efforts finally arrived when the huge door creaked open, only enough for me to see the sliver of a disgruntled face through the crack. Coughing just a little as if to reset the tone of this conversation, I handed over the hatstand, which was received with a mixture of surprise and confusion, and a mumbled thanks, before the door was curtly closed in my face. Coin Lady turned to me with a big, radiant smile, and with unmanufactured innocence asked me why it was so important for me to return a hatstand on a morning when the shop wasn't open until midday.

31

Auctions

I WAS STANDING IN the basement of an auction house, feeling bad for trampling muck all over their expensive carpet. I'd eventually been admitted by the doorman, who was wearing a top hat in what seemed like a ludicrous commercial pretension, but only after he'd quizzed me for a not insignificant amount of time as to the nature of my visit. I couldn't help but notice he didn't stop the lady with the expensive jewellery from going inside, nor the busy-looking chap in a cravat. I think he took issue with my cardigan.

We'd purchased a book from one of the sales, and I'd been sent to collect it. Even after the altercation with the doorman, I sauntered inside with all the confidence of a person who has never been sent to collect anything from an expensive auction house before. The interior was a maze of unhelpful signs and mood lighting, with the mood of the day being disapproval. It took me twenty-five minutes to find the right counter, because I got lost on the second concentric staircase and almost wandered into an auction for uncannily realistic sculptures.

The counter was manned by a tired-looking gentleman

with a Lithuanian accent who gave off the impression he'd been lifting heavy things since the early hours of the morning and did not want to lift any more. He was, by merit of that attitude, the only sympathetic person I'd met so far inside the auction house. I explained why I was present, and he cut me off to inform me that in order to collect the book, I needed a special numbered key which would be provided to me at a desk in the basement on the other side of the auction house.

Grumbling, I picked up my things and made my way back through the winding corridors, past the suspicious auction room, gave a wave to the angry doorman, bumped into two women wheeling away a hideous vase, and went down into the basement. In the half light, a single staff member was barricaded behind glass in a secure booth that quite evidently had seats for at least four more staff, and which could probably have held off anything short of a battering ram. Pretending not to notice me was a seated woman with an expression imperious enough to be stamped on to the back of a coin, and she refused to acknowledge me until I pressed the little bell in front of her face.

I gave her the grimace I'd prepared, and laid out my paperwork for her, explaining what I was here to collect.

She nodded, reluctantly, and I waited an hour in the otherwise empty room as she shuffled papers in front of my face. Eventually she reached a decision. 'I'm dreadfully sorry, but you aren't on the authorized list for collections.'

I was perplexed. 'Well, I need to collect this book. So how do I get my name on the list?'

She unveiled a grin which was all canines. 'Your

company already has an authorized list. You'll need some-one already on that list to sign this form.'

I took a look at the list of people who could authorize me. 'I'm sorry, there's been a mistake.' I hesitantly laughed. 'None of these people are alive any more.'

The woman's face scrolled through several equally inscrutable expressions before she landed on her stance. 'You can change the authorized names,' she said, slowly, but with increasing confidence, 'if you have a signature from one of the people already on the authorized list.'

'Madam,' I repeated, 'they are dead. None of these people can sign anything.'

She looked at me. I looked at her. I resolved not to leave until I had acquired the book, and prepared myself for a drawn-out encounter. Surely, I thought, the system couldn't work like this. She'd probably just misunderstood the rules. I asked to speak to someone else, which was a mistake because a near-identical lady appeared from the back with surprising dexterity and started at the very beginning.

'Oh, I see the problem,' she said, cleaning her glasses with a dirty cloth. 'Yes, you see the authorized names are all deceased.'

I gritted my teeth. 'Yes,' I said. 'But I need to collect the book.'

She left another pregnant pause, and blinked a few times, slowly. 'Oh dear.' She shook her head, pushing my paperwork back at me. 'We really do need a signature from one of them before we can proceed.' Then her face lit up, as if she'd had a great idea. 'I'll go and fetch someone else, hold on.'

Two supervisors, one manager and seven internal phone calls later, a group of confused staff members had gathered into a single booth. The main attendant dropped the veneer of friendliness about half an hour in, and the others simply looked like they were respectively avoiding some less pleasant business somewhere else in the auction house. The problem had to be explained all over again every time new help arrived. At six o'clock I was informed that they were awfully sorry, but they were closing. I did not leave with the book.

32

York

IF ALL ROADS lead to Rome, then all English bookselling eventually leads you back to York. There is, I am sure, some well-known intricacy of English history which explains the quirk, but York has (or remains) a national hub of antiquarian bookselling, with far more than its fair share of rare bookshops. Book fairs take place there each year which rival those of London in scope, if not surpassing them entirely, and it's something of a pilgrimage for many booksellers to make their way there each year and enjoy the olde worlde feel of the city. Even more than London, York is invested with the truest of antiquarian aesthetics, retaining the kind of winding street and creaking old shopfront that London loves to replace with office blocks. I recall once being shanghaied into a local dive called the 'House of Trembling Madness', said to be very popular with booksellers on tour, in which you are surrounded by a thousand taxidermied animal heads. The bar is hidden, so you are unlikely to stumble across it unless you know it's already there, making it the perfect haunt for a bookseller looking to avoid customers, bailiffs or lawyers. I have often advocated for Sotheran's to take this approach, as I am sure we could find some adventurous architect willing to obscure our entrance behind a towering pile of rocks, or disguise our vestibule to look like a disused building site.* But I digress.

It came to pass that the Antiquarian Book Association, who had been part-funding my apprenticeship, decided that it would be very nice if I should attend the rare book seminar that takes place annually in York. The seminar is a rather recent idea designed to try and encourage more people to get into the trade, and more importantly I never say no to a free sandwich. You wouldn't think it would be easy to encourage a bunch of booksellers to come together in a room for lectures and questions, reclusive as they are, but I think the opportunity to spend an hour or two excitedly talking about their very specific area of interest serves to tempt them. Now, I'd never been to York before, but Sotheran's was paying for my room and board and it meant a few days off the shop floor, so I determined to treat it like a mini holiday. I was handed a company card (with some

---

* In the spirit of Douglas Adams, I have long yearned for a 'Beware of the Leopard' sign to place near my desk in order to deter customers.

consternation on Evelyn's part) and told to book myself a
room somewhere.*

I tried to be abstemious in my choice of hotel, which is
how I ended up crammed into a tiny box room in the back
of an old lady's house which smelled like the colour brown,
somewhere in the reaches of York and (very importantly)
nowhere near where I needed to be. If you hadn't already
gathered, it should be becoming clear to you just how bad
I am at planning excursions. The room next to me was
occupied by a guest I never met; I was left to assume, from
the hissing and shuffling, that I was sharing lodgings with a
salamander. The lady from whom I was renting the room
did provide breakfast, should one be carrying cash, but I
caught a glimpse of the kitchen on the way through and
decided that hungry was better than dead. She engaged me
in brief conversation only long enough to complain bitterly
about 'bookseller season' or something to that effect (a dialogue I had no incentive to prolong) so I hastily took my
leave.

It was just as well that I skipped breakfast, because I had
to leave rather early in the morning. On checking the map,
I'd discovered that the sightseeing walk I had planned
might instead have to be more of a light jog. I had a slight

---

* To this day, I am only very rarely afforded the privilege of using a company credit card. There seems to be some general reluctance to give me
access to that much impromptu unvetted spending power. I think there's
some fear that I might spend it all on creepy unsaleable books, which on a
certain level I resent and on another level I completely understand, because
that is exactly what I would do.

sense of déjà vu as I clambered across a dilapidated railway bridge,* but I arrived (drenched in my own shame) just in time to grab a seat at the back of the class and pull out a notebook.

I was not a star pupil in my youth, for lots of reasons including a kneejerk resistance to authority, but chiefly because my narcolepsy set in when I was in my teens and caused me to haze over whenever I was left in a calm, sedate situation, such as listening to a well-meaning bookseller talk softly about calming things in a dimly lit room for several hours. In all the excitement of dragging myself halfway to Scotland, this important fact had completely slipped by me, and only came to mind as I began to doze off during the first lecture, which was something very useful about reference books I was doomed to miss.

To either side of me, as I took an ill-earned nap at the back of class, eager rare book students studiously made notes. It was an odd collection of characters – though I'm not sure who else one might expect to see at a rare book seminar. The room couldn't have held more than thirty students, but the motley diversity of the people who wanted to be involved was oddly motivating. On one side, a retired judge with a strigine expression looking for some way to pass the

---

* If you intend to pursue a career with rare books in England, I feel obliged to point out that you will spend an inordinate amount of time navigating disused railway bridges. I'm not sure precisely what causes book collectors and dealers to gravitate towards them, but you had better bring sturdy shoes, and if you have a fear of sudden drops over twisting expanses of rusty metal you might as well forget it.

time, frequently throwing the instructors a withering look that threatened to disembowel them mid-lecture. In front of me, a collection of torturously well-dressed young booksellers from one high-end shop or another who had already formed a clique. To my other side, however, was crouched a gigantic tattooed Welshman who took up the space of about three booksellers, and seemed to interpret my regular snoozes as some kind of anarchic rebellious statement. Down with the man, and so on. I was quickly (and reluctantly) embraced into the nightmarish fold of his affections, and between lectures he began to fill me in on the various underhand ways you stayed in business as a rural book dealer in the hinterlands. It was at this point that I should have said something, but I have a weakness for tight shirts so I let him believe that I was some kind of maverick while he detailed precisely how one might go about hotwiring a car with one arm full of books.

The lectures ranged on throughout the day, each time with a new kind of bookseller drifting up to the front to talk about their very specific area of interest. Some were clearly natural teachers, others looked like they were there under duress, performing in a wide-eyed state of understated panic, as if to avoid some terrible fate befalling their loved ones. One chap would occasionally break off from what he was saying entirely and just stare wistfully at the door until someone prompted him to continue. In between lectures, I gathered that the community of antiquarian booksellers was annually harvested for this course, with various favours and debts called in to encourage people to come and share their knowledge with the up and coming. For all that some might have seemed reluctant on the surface, whispered words and quiet asides made it very clear that among the booksellers there was a very real fear that the antiquarian bookselling tradition might die off if new blood could not be sourced and fed to the industry. A fear pressing enough to collect a little parliament of socially agnostic booksellers together into one room so they could talk in front of a crowd.

Passing from person to person like a discarded bookmark, I chatted to a few groups of students, and I think if the professors had heard some of the conversations they would have been less worried. There's a hunger about book people, about anyone who gets involved with old books. To follow a path so peculiar, with so few opportunities, and with no real prospects for wealth or prestige, I think you have to have a fickle relationship with rationality. James used to say that the Sotheran's motto should be 'You don't have to be mad to work here, but it helps'. There will always, to my mind, be people odd enough to get involved in rare bookselling, and I think what really matters is that as shopfronts close and older booksellers develop increasingly reclusive business models, booksellers find ways like the York seminars to pass on their knowledge. The rest, I think, will take care of itself.

33

3D Tetris

I HAD PLENTY OF time to study my bookselling materials on the train, because a bookseller is always hurtling to one location or another via locomotive. I was on the way to a house in the suburbs, some mansion or other where an infrequent client of ours had told us they wished to dispense with their collection. I was in a hurry because I was certain Rebekah was already waiting for me there.

We hired Rebekah because, or so I thought at the time, Literature is quite a large subject area and it requires multiple booksellers to manage the sheer volume of content. I have since revised my opinion to reflect that it requires either multiple booksellers to manage it or a single Rebekah. I wasn't present for the interview, so I can't imagine what was said, but I don't think anyone predicted exactly what had been set into motion. The thing about Rebekah is that she works hard. She hadn't been in the seat for a week before she'd completed a cataloguing task Andrew had left uncompleted for twenty years, and which I had inherited, leaving undone for the better part of another decade. When it was handed to her (me thinking I had outsmarted the task by passing it on to someone else who would ignore it the same way I had), she did it that very afternoon. Fundamentally, she seems to actually rather *like* bookselling, in comparison to my wary tolerance of it. Together, we make rather a balanced team.

It's not uncommon for booksellers to tackle collections in pairs, though Rebekah and I are more accustomed than most to doing it because we both work with literature. Sometimes a collection is too large for a single bookseller to handle, or you get a phone call from someone who sounds like they might lock you up in a castle with their enchanted crockery, so you want back-up. Regardless, it's nice to have someone to talk to, ask opinions of, and lament over particularly tragic books with.

The house Rebekah and I were visiting was modestly appointed, and the gentleman welcomed us with a cup of tea. (A note to anyone who wishes to sell books: if you want your bookseller in a good mood – and more importantly, a buying mood – fortifying them with tea is essential.) We discussed his books, and as minutes turned into an hour I began to wonder if he would ever show us to the library. Rebekah had a notepad out, which I thought was admirable because the closest I've ever come to a notepad is a commonplace book in which I make doodles while looking attentive.

Eventually he ran out of excuses and showed us to a room packed with books along one wall. His wife wanted him to get rid of them, he told us sadly, so they could downsize and move to a smaller house. It didn't sound like he agreed with the idea. He showed us a number of further rooms, each of which contained cases and cases of increasingly disorganized books. Some of the rooms were completely inaccessible as books filled the doorframe in such a manner that he could only have achieved it by strategically filling the gaps as he retreated, like a three-dimensional game of Tetris. I felt less and less sympathetic for his position as I hopped over stacks of books, trying not to send any of the piles tumbling, lest I cause an avalanche.

After four hours of work we'd managed to sort through a single bookcase in one of the rooms, isolating some volumes we'd whisk back to the shop for appraisal. He looked reproachful at first, but brightened when he realized that we were out of time to go through the rest. Bustling us out of the house, he thanked us for coming and promised us we could come back and look at the rest another time.

After paying him for the books we'd taken, we tried contacting him again, but we have never received another invitation.

34

Dungeoneering

I'D BEEN WORKING at Sotheran's about a year before I heard about the Other Cellars. At the time, they were solely the purview of the looming James, who knew all the company secrets worth knowing, and acted as their quiet custodian. But eventually it came to pass that someone without creaky knees was needed to shift some items from inside them, and thus I was inducted into the mystery of the Other Cellars at King's Cross. It was made clear to me that the Other Cellars were not to be taken lightly, and neither were they to be idly tampered with. They were another fey world, and James was the jealous Erlkönig of this subterranean lair. Oddly, no one seemed to have any interest in the Other Cellars, except on the rare occasion that James should be commanded to retrieve some object of importance, lest it disappear for ever.

As the chronicles record, back in the distant twentieth century, Sotheran's decided it would be a wonderful idea to buy out a fading architectural bookseller called Weinreb – this wasn't uncommon practice, particularly if a bookseller of good renown was retiring – and take on all of their stock. All of it. As you will no doubt have gathered by now, a respectable antiquarian bookseller develops quite the hoard of irrelevancies, knick-knacks and oddments over the course of a successful career, and Sotheran's blithely agreed to give them cash for the whole lot. I am sure that Weinreb is laughing in his grave to this day. I suppose that the Sotheran's staff of the age were of the opinion that the bad Weinreb books could be holed up in the cellars somewhere far away and it would be decades before anyone noticed. This, it transpired, was absolutely true. When the good books had been removed from Weinreb's stock and sold, the rest were sent to the Other Cellars, there to languish in eternal torment. Whatever noble ephemera had once occupied the cellars, the Weinreb detritus drowned it in doorstoppers dealing with architectural minutiae. Since then, despite various forays with industrial machinery, the Other Cellars have become a muddled repository for things banished from the shop floor. For a book, being consigned to the Other Cellars is tantamount to a death sentence.

Nevertheless, sometimes duty requires that some long-forgotten book thought completely unsaleable be retrieved from the cellars, and in cases such as this someone has to make the unpleasant journey down into the dark. London streets being what they are in the West End, you can reach the Other Cellars through a number of routes. In my opinion it's quickest to zip through the gay district of Soho and out the other side into a disused restaurant loading dock behind a theatre, though I know Chris prefers to dodge through a sinister park, and Stephen the furbisher likes to wander past a particular row of old shopfronts which I never seem to be able to find when I'm not with him. Georg changes his route every time, and though I've never seen her go there, I suspect Rebekah would take the longest route possible, as she seems incorrigibly fond of walking. James would sometimes call them the Cellars at King's Cross, which was very unhelpful because they are not anywhere near King's Cross, and if you're confused by that then you're following along just fine. You can also drive, in theory, though you really should shun this option if you want to avoid being trapped in a one-way system until your body withers into a husk.

Once in that strange, abandoned street, you'll need to locate a block of flats constructed during one of London's social housing drives many years ago. It looks abandoned, but it isn't quite. With the right key you can get past the outer doors and into the bleak stone antechamber, in which faded signs reading BEWARE OF THIEF are still peeling off the brickwork. People still live there, I assume, because someone is taking very good care of the plants. You sometimes hear creaking sounds from the flats above, and if you wait long enough a resident will flutter by over your head, casting a vastly disproportionate shadow.

To access the cellars, one must find the door downwards, a skeletal black grille sealed by a slightly broken padlock.* If you know the trick, you can use an unlikely-looking key to crack open the lock and remove the grille – and one must always take the padlock down into the dark, because otherwise some unknown person will come along and seal the gate behind you. The padlock is significantly harder to unlock from the other side, I'll tell you that much, but let us be thankful I have dexterous hands, or I might still be down there. The staircase is a stone spiral down into the dark. There are no lights, but presuming one was sensible enough to head to the cellars during the day, the fading grey light will illuminate the first curve far enough for the intrepid bookseller to get their bearings. At the bottom, an alcove containing abandoned tools of unknown purpose, and a subterranean underpass leading to an enclosed corridor with an open roof. It's usually wet down there – some leak or blocked drain that's covered the floor with a stagnant puddle and made the brickwork damp. Sometimes the puddle takes on festive colours. I have no explanation for that. Shadowed windows and doors covered in peeling dark blue paint are spaced evenly along the tunnel wall, and the very last of these leads to the Sotheran's cellar. A third key opens the intimidating padlock here, and the door swings inwards into the vault.

The first thing that hits you is the smell. Decades of books closely stacked on top of each other without ever being touched leaves a distinctive and slightly violent odour

---

* I am often asked to go to the cellars because I am one of the only people who can use this particular padlock. There's a knack to it, a twist of the wrist at just the right moment.

behind, even if you later remove the books or shift the shelves around. The Other Cellars are steeped in it, which means as soon as you remove the padlock and creak open the door, it smacks you in the face and steals your wallet. Despite many concerted efforts to clear the Other Cellars of detritus over the years, it never lasts more than a few weeks before mess creeps back in. Ratty boxes. Shredded bookbindings. Errant illustrations dragged off to a dark corner and used as nests.* Webs hang from every corner and wall, in places the strands so dust-laden that they seem more like curtains, or decorative rope arrangements. In the distant past, some helpful soul provided rows of iron shelving to store the books on, which have slowly rusted over the years to add to the ambience. To find anything, you have to hop over the first few rows of books (checking carefully for supernaturally large spiders) and root about the shelving with intent. Nothing is labelled.

Now, over the years I have rarely been fortunate enough to attend the Other Cellars with company. It's not usually a job that requires more than one bookseller unless some large number of books is being moved. It's an eerie job, because there's only one light switch in the room (a dull orange bulb hanging from a negligent tangle of wiring) and it's guarded

---

* I have never seen a mouse or a rat in the cellars, which is surprising given the abundance of nesting materials. Privately I have come to believe that this is for one of two reasons: either the mice (glutted on resources) have developed their society to the stage where they are organized in their subterfuge, or there's something nasty in the cellars which the mice would rather stay away from.

by a ferocious and disturbingly territorial arachnid that I am reluctant to agitate in case one day it decides to move on from a diet of bookworms. Usually one uses a torch for a quick rummage in the dark, with the goal being to execute the mission as swiftly as possible so you can leave the wretched place behind. However, in the hustle of opening up and the unnerving rush of sorting through boxes as quickly as possible, it's easy to forget about the Cellar Lady.

I call her the Cellar Lady because I don't remember her name, but I have since been reliably informed that she does have one. One of the doors down there is hers, and it has a little box nearby for people to put letters in. They say that she lives down there, and always has done, though no one thought to warn me of this until I discovered her for myself as I was working through boxes by torchlight. I am used to dismissing the autonomous rustles of boxes and papers as vaguely supernatural, perhaps attributable to a Ristlestig, but not worth investigating, so when a disapproving voice sounded from the shadows – 'Who Are You?' – my heart almost stopped beating as I jumped a foot in the air and scattered books all over the place. My head was suddenly full of all the times I'd told myself that I was imagining noises, when I'd assured myself that I was alone. Irrational images of gigantic spiders and box monsters sprang unbidden to mind.

She had to ask again before she got anything close to a straight answer out of me, because (still in fight-or-flight mode) I was instinctively searching my surroundings for something I could use as a weapon. She wasn't tall, and had the air of a person who knew what *she* was doing there, but wasn't sure why I was in her way. 'Who Are You?' she said again, this time with a note of impatience. Somehow, I mustered a little courage, and told her my name.

'This cellar belongs to a bookshop,' she noted, as if she had caught me in the perpetration of something undesirable. 'This is Sotheran's cellar.'

I found myself on the defensive. 'Well, I work there,' I said, feebly (covered in grime and about twenty years younger than the average Sotheran's staff member).

'Work there, do you?' she repeated dubiously. She eyed me keenly. 'I don't know you.'

I couldn't dispute the fact, and even if I had wanted to, my mind was still focused on remembering all the occasions I had been here before on my own. Had she been here then, too? How many times had I wandered in the dark, unknowingly a hair's breadth from this mysterious woman? Had she seen the time I'd stopped to have lunch down here? Should I have offered her some? I was adrift when it came to the etiquette for a cellar encounter.

She seemed to take pity on me in my helplessness. 'Should be careful down here,' she said. 'Should hold on to that lock when you come inside, too.' She pointed at the rusty padlock I had carelessly left near the doorway. 'Could be stuck down here, otherwise. Thieves about, don't you know.' I nodded mutely, and she seemed to take this as a kind of understanding between us, heading to her door, shaking her head. I had missed my chance to impress her, and as I stepped out into the light it became clear that she was just a nice lady trying to give me advice about getting locked in.

Embarrassed, I rushed back to the shop with my tail between my legs. Thinking that I could at the very least get some validation from my colleagues, I breathlessly recounted the ordeal to Andrew, who was unperturbed. This seemed very uncharitable of him (I was sure I had made it sound very dramatic) so I tried again with James, who informed me in the exasperated tone he adopted when I was taking too long to grasp a new concept that of course a woman lived down in the cellars, and that I should be more polite to her in future.

It was a few months ago that we discovered the Other Other Cellar. When looking at our financial records, it fell to Evelyn to gently but firmly remind everyone in her way that we were in fact paying for two cellars down in the dark, and to politely wonder aloud if we were still using the second one. Naturally, no one had any firm recollection of there even being a second cellar.

Thus the hunt began for the key. Drawers were opened, keyrings assessed. Likely candidates were selected, and an expedition party was formed. A short scenic walk later, and we got lucky with one of our keys, creaking open a door which hadn't been used in decades. The room was filled with dust, and I would be lying if I said I wasn't hoping for undiscovered treasures, or at least a box of scandalous letters. Instead, we found the following: a plastic basin (half submerged in dank water); a series of sinister empty portrait frames; and a large filing cabinet full of papers that belonged to a rival bookshop. All in all, it had the air of a thirty-year-old heist gone wrong.

35

To a Certain Degree

WHEN I TOLD my friends and family that I was entering the world of rare books, I don't think the image in their minds included me shoulder-barging my way into filthy abandoned cellars. Certainly, after several years of an apprenticeship, they at least expected me to be wearing tweed, and perhaps even be earning enough to rent my own apartment. My mother had her reservations about my choice of vocation, and it was very difficult to argue with her from under a pile of books. No doubt she considered it better than me returning with my tail between my legs to cause a mess under her roof, but I think she had envisioned somewhat greater things for me than the penniless life of an old bookseller. The root of the problem, as she seemed to see it, was my lack of higher education, which meant that no matter how experienced I became, I couldn't move on from a bookshop to something more respectable like a library. There were reasons I never pursued this path – my undiagnosed narcolepsy caused a cascade of exam 'failures' which lost me all my secured university places, the very same turn of events which caused me to find my way to an apprenticeship in the first place. At the time there was nothing to be done about it, and I was quite happy to bumble along as I always have without ever looking back over my shoulder at the spectre of academia.

Just as soon as I'd been at Sotheran's long enough to find my feet and start feeling like I might finally be getting a grip on things, the questions started about what my prospects were from here, and I didn't really have the heart to say that there were no prospects whatsoever, that this particular career path involved being impoverished until I died of scurvy or something.

The problem was a misconception, at heart. Anyone on the outside of the rare book world would think (quite reasonably) that experience in a rare bookshop would be a leg-up in the world of institutions like libraries or archives. It's not a silly assumption, and people are often quite surprised when they discover that most branches on the rare book tree require their own very specialized set of qualifications before you can even take a running jump at them. Of all the avenues into handling books, rare bookselling has the fewest barriers to entry, has very little oversight, and the average institution considers experience at a rare bookshop about as valuable as experience in a coal mine if you can't also produce a relevant advanced degree in something like Library Sciences or Museum Adjacent Skulduggery. I made the mistake of mentioning this in conversation, and the idea of my taking another shot at academia raised its ugly head.

I held out for a year or so before caving, resentfully stalking the internet for something I could pursue while not giving up my independence. For all that I was barely being paid enough to rent a box room from a friend of mine,* the

---

* A room in which I could not stand up straight due to the slanted ceiling. I believe its original purpose was something akin to a coal shed. I still stay there when I'm in the area because I developed a fondness for it, and my hosts make excellent food, and because ever since I moved out the place is much cleaner.

hard-won independence was something I was loath to relinquish, and so if I were to take on study it would have to be on top of my work at Sotheran's. Ideally something relevant. I suspect you are beginning to see the problem, because there are a limited number of flexible, cheap university courses within walking distance of Sotheran's which would be specifically useful to someone in the rare book trade.

But there was *one*.

The Institute of English Studies, located an energetic stone's throw away in Bloomsbury, provided a master's degree programme in the History of the Book, a niche course for which I was not at all eligible given my lack of a bachelor's degree. This made it a perfect target, because I could make a believable attempt at entry, fail on a technicality, and then everyone would be satisfied that I had tried my best. Alas, my very devious plan neglected to take into account two things. The first was that I have an uncanny knack for stumbling into success at unlikely moments, and the second was Cynthia.

When I contacted the university, I sincerely expected to be rebuffed without a by-your-leave. And I think at any other institution I would have been. As my luck would have it, my polite email asking for an interview landed on Cynthia's desk, and as she remains a law unto herself she asked me to come down and chat to her, which is where things began to spiral out of control.

The Institute of English Studies is located in the towering art deco monument to Babel otherwise known as Senate House, situated in the leafy university district of Bloomsbury. It's a beautiful place even in the dregs of autumn, and the first thing I noticed as I stepped through that door into the atrium was the hush. A hush that might have subdued or intimidated me if I hadn't heard it before every day as I came into work. This was the Sotheran's hush, that strange, oppressive atmosphere generated around scholarly people who want nothing more than to be left alone with books but are doomed to interact with members of the public. If anything, the atmosphere gave me a perverse sense of confidence. I found my way to Cynthia's office after walking around a maze of identical-looking rooms stacked high with reference books and people clearly hoping I was not about to interrupt them. By this stage I had already decided that this was the right place for me to cobble together an education, as clearly I was among kindred spirits.

How does one describe Cynthia? I don't think I can do her justice. Cynthia was, and is, everything I love about the world of rare books distilled into one person, a mantle which she bears with grace. I don't know what I really thought about academia before I met her, but I had definitely convinced myself on some level that it would always be inaccessible to me. Softly but firmly spoken, and with a dry turn of phrase, there was always a slight shake of the head to Cynthia's tone of voice as if there were some vastly amusing joke to it all which only she knew the secret of. It's that feeling you get when you meet someone with whom you share a deep affinity, in my case someone who understood that (a) everything is a bother, and (b) sometimes the bother is absolutely worth it.

The winding process which brought me to graduation could perhaps fill its own memoir, but the sum of the matter is it took four years for me to laboriously complete a course that should have been done in two, with Cynthia intervening almost every step of the way to accommodate late essays, last-minute tutorials and advice long past the point where her duties to me had been discharged and I had officially overstayed my welcome.

I am a poor academic, with the same flagrant disregard for scholarly convention which makes me a rather good bookseller. Nevertheless I worked in the evenings, and at weekends. I worked on my holidays, and in between customers. I worked hard for possibly the first time in my life, and my effort was repaid in kind. It was Cynthia who quietly passed me a form for a scholarship that ended up paying all my fees. I have no doubt it was Cynthia who convinced admissions to overlook my glaring lack of qualifications.* Finally, it was Cynthia who stepped on the right departments to grant me not one but two extra years in which to drag my sorry, weather-beaten carcass over the finish line.

In the present day I am the proud owner of a master's degree, a mark of hard-won expertise which I brought back to Sotheran's knowing there was zero chance this would result in a pay rise.

---

* I should mention that Cynthia was not the only tutor who went out of their way to provide me with extra notes, or lend me books from their own personal collection. All in all the entire faculty for the History of the Book programme operated with a wicked glee which I recognized from my colleagues, and made me feel very much at home.

Barn owl, somewhat deceased but still good. Faded in places, but skilfully preserved. Decorative bell jar provided at no extra charge.

NATURAL HISTORY

A bestiary comprising specimens frequently encountered, diverse specimens catalogued and assorted literary grotesqueries.

NATURAL HISTORY IS a capacious category covering anything which crawls, flies or swims, in addition to anything vaguely scientific. You'll have to forgive us for that. A seventeenth-century book on bedbugs and *A Brief History of Time* might seem like very different books to you, but to Sotheran's they are essentially the same book at different levels of magnification.

36

Parties

CONTRARY TO POPULAR belief, and maybe surprisingly given how I've represented booksellers so far, Sotheran's is no stranger to an after-hours soirée. If I've intimated in any way that the Powers who own the bookshop are unattainably distant, then I should correct myself here, because very infrequently they sweep into Sotheran's for parties and book launches.

It's my belief that anyone worth knowing enjoys spending time in a bookshop. I may be biased, but I can't think of a more pleasant place to spend one's time. The floor space and quiet make them suitable for all kinds of events and functions, even if they might not always be strictly book-related. Further, if you're of the means to do so then it stands to reason that you would make good use of the highly atmospheric antiquarian bookshop that you happen to own for this very purpose. If I owned a bookshop, I imagine I would do exactly that (as often as I could force myself to socialize).

The Powers have always had a very generous idea of how these events will pan out, and on every occasion they politely requested that the booksellers staff the event, almost as if they were suffering from some kind of severe amnesia.

If this book has taught you anything about the kinds of people who end up in the rare book industry, then I am sure you can appreciate how everyone reacted to being asked to provide a drinks service, collect coats and generally tidy up ahead of a swanky event – which is to say, there was almost no reaction at all, and everyone pretended that it wasn't happening until a few hours before the party. I think the Powers were convinced on each occasion that *this* time the bookshop would be prepared, which seems to me a very destructive kind of optimism.

Before the guests arrived for each event, the shop had to be neutralized of the more obvious threats, and a sweep of the place was executed to remove or hide some of the more dangerous shop equipment. Ladders and heavy books were resituated where they could not fall and crush a guest.* Rogue craft knives were stashed in drawers. Incorrect name badges were dispersed among the staff. Depending on the event, and which badge I grabbed from my drawer, I might be Mike, or perhaps Daisy. Boxes were poorly concealed under tables, some of them sticking out into walkways like booby traps.

Most importantly, books and artefacts were retrieved from all over the shop. If you've ever been in receipt of an unwanted knick-knack from a relative you could not afford to insult, you might recognize this particular stratagem. Depending on the guest list, a variety of never-before-seen

---

* There is something about geriatric men which attracts them to dangerous ladders. Unless you are very careful to hide anything with steps, you invariably end up shouting 'Mr Beekman, please come down' to a cackling octogenarian daredevil as he teeters above a deadly three-foot fall.

items would emerge from hiding, such as copies of books written by the guests (or their close family) and donated to the shop many years previously. Huge champagne bottles, none of which ever remained full for long. Some items needed to be hidden, because they had been abandoned at a previous party, and no one wanted to have the conversation about why we'd held on to them for so long without confronting the owner.

In the flurry before such an event, James would always make a point of mentioning that a Sotheran's party was the kind of elegant, discreet engagement people would swan over to at 5 p.m. before leaving for dinner at 7. This was important to him because it meant we had to close the bookshop an hour early to accommodate it, something he nursed a quiet resentment over if his dark muttering was any indication.

At around 4.55 p.m., guests would begin to arrive, tentatively stepping inside as if they weren't sure if they were in the right location. You only turn up early to a Sotheran's event once before you learn better. Because it wasn't 5 p.m. yet, guests were often left to circumperambulate in a nervous manner until the bell struck the hour, at which point James would swoop down on them insisting they divest themselves of their hats. If the only hatstand in bookselling had been acquired from Jarndyce, then someone might have set it up on the lower floor out of sight, requiring the guests to go in search of it. Most of them would decide to clutch their belongings close to them instead, quite rightly fearing that if they put down their gigantic hats for more than a moment, they might never see them again.

As more guests arrived, opportunistic and unrelated customers would filter in. There was rarely a sign up at any of these events explaining that they were private, so the eventuality was a foregone conclusion. The fatal arrival of impromptu clients, clouds of bemused tourists and the occasional cryptid, made for an enjoyable mix of terrified guests and predatory regulars, many of the latter turning up simply for the free wine and a captive audience. In the lead-up to any event, some small effort was always directed to ensuring potential otherworldly gate-crashers had no idea the party was taking place, though one inevitably found that the Spindleman had somehow burrowed inside and cornered the Duke of Casterbridge in an attempt to sell him a hideous book of copperplate engravings.

On top of all this, the guests had the booksellers to contend with. It's not that booksellers are dirty, per se, because by and large we are not. There is, however, a weathering of the soul that comes with the profession, a sort of fraying at the edges which is visible even if one has managed to find a half-decent tie being used as a bookmark inside *A History of English Craft Bookbinding*. With time and exposure to books, your average antiquarian bookseller slowly loses any shiny veneer they once possessed, leaving behind something that's a bit shabby but very authentic. This is all a roundabout way of saying that forcing a bunch of antiquarian booksellers to play host at your fancy event is a bit like inviting the Queen to a monster truck rally – entertaining, but somehow unbecoming.

Over the years, the Powers have slowly stopped trying to engage Sotheran's staff in events, and though this is probably for the best it is a little sad to think that I'll never again be able to slowly lower the grille while a bunch of people run about trying to find their fur coats and dive under it before I lock up and go home.

37

Kerfuffles

WHEN VIOLENCE STRIKES, one never really knows how one will react until one is placed on the spot. You have grand delusions about being firm with people, or facing down an intruder with nothing but a sharpened bookmark, but in truth it's not something you expect to deal with at an antiquarian bookshop.

We don't often see unaccompanied teens in Sotheran's. Well, we do, but we get the kind of youth with book lust burning in their expression and bad eyesight from too many hours squinting at texts under the covers – the kind of teen you can leave alone to do a wide-eyed, silent tour of the place without worrying about flash photography or loud conversation. Any other kind of unaccompanied child, particularly those looking for trouble, sticks out like a sore thumb. Much like adults, very few are brave enough to enter the deathly quiet of a bookshop and make a racket when faced with the withering glares of every bookseller they encounter.

So it was that I began to inhabit a false sense of security. For all the strange creatures and stranger customers that haunt the shop, there is rarely any real sense of urgency or threat. The closest thing to an emergency in day-to-day life involves whether you've accidentally sold a book to two different people, and even then you have a day or two to mull over how to handle it.* This prelapsarian calm was stripped from me one afternoon when a loud ruckus from the street penetrated the quiet, agitated shadows. The voices, arguing in thick Irish accents, were clearly upset about something very dear to them, and were heading towards the shop in a gently rotating circular manner, like two boxers getting the measure of each other. I caught a glimpse of James reaching for the Irish Box.†

The door crashed open to admit a pair of yelling teenagers, in that stage of life when everything is gangles and angry noises, already immersed in the prelude of an emerging altercation where no party had yet found the correct opening in the music to launch their first fist, but which had clearly descended past the point of no return into the realm of insulting each other's mothers. The pair of them barged through the swinging door in a whirlwind of lilting profanity, and the rising tenor of the conversation made it very clear that combat was inevitable.

To their credit, the two belligerents recovered exceptionally quickly from the stultifying hush that usually stops people

---

* You give the book to the person you like more.

† Amid the many contingencies James prepared for, he kept a small chest of Irish materials, authors, maps and ephemera. It was never adequately explained to me why Ireland should receive such a special consideration (or possibly quarantine), and it was surprising how often it came into use.

in their tracks. Ordinarily, anyone with the nerve to walk in screaming at the top of their lungs would have been paralysed by the echoing silence all around them, but the spirit of war lent them strength and they headed right in my direction. Suddenly, at my tiny desk in front of the stairs, right in the way of the front door, I became aware of my role as First Line of Defence. Until this moment there had been no call for me to fulfil this duty. It came to me in a flash, as fate barrelled towards me over the threshold, that I had been in a blissful state of denial about what a job in retail might entail.

Time froze. I took a long while to consider if it would be an intelligent use of my time and effort to get in the way and intervene in the developing disaster. Moments stretched by as I considered what I had been taught, and the example my colleagues had set for me. I thought about the legacy of Sotheran's, about the proud tradition of bookselling, and my responsibilities towards my employer.

Reader, I got out of the way. I faded into the background with an alacrity I think James would have appreciated if he hadn't been rooting about under a pile of Conrads looking for the Irish Box. The quarrellers had begun their fracas in earnest, one chasing the other towards the stairwell. Why they chose to do so eludes me. It didn't even seem to cross their minds that everyone was staring at them. As soon as the duo hurtled past me and down on to the lower floor, everyone visibly relaxed, as if what happened on another floor might as well be on another plane of existence. The two were, I think, expecting a similar lack of resistance to that which they had encountered upstairs, but instead they met Richard.

Though Sotheran's is a bookshop, it's also a gallery space and a seller of prints going back into the distant past. There was even a time, lost now to memory, when they operated a standalone print gallery, but these days we run a more discreet operation from the basement level. Richard, who takes some measure of responsibility for the department, has cases and cases of peculiar prints, illustrations and posters which decorate many of the walls and break up the otherwise endless cases of books with some much-needed colour. If it seems strange that he hasn't really come up before now, consider that he rather sensibly tries to keep out of the way of books as much as possible. Unlike everyone else in the shop, Richard keeps meticulous track of all his posters. All his drawers are labelled. When a sale is made, he writes out a little envelope with all the information inside. It's like something out of a parallel world where people make notes, keep track of their stock and generally have a grip on their lives.

Richard can be found at his well-organized desk in front of the posters, scribbling notes, measuring things precisely, or sometimes hunting down the various stationery items other people have stolen from him.* Very little can rouse Richard from this post, other than the gentlemanly urge to make everyone tea: he finds it very difficult to make himself tea without first offering it to anyone else working in the shop, a favour which in many long years I have never once returned. I have a lurking fear that he's actually storing up

---

* It's me. I'm that person.

some huge favour which will be called in when I least expect it, a favour worth a thousand teas.

On the occasion that he finds a reason to depart his desk, he's one of those people who is much taller than you'd expect. Of all the staff, I think he's the most consistently hard to rattle, taking everything in his stride and resolutely impossible to catch off guard. I think it's possible he missed his calling as a horse whisperer, or maybe a cult leader. When he says something to you, it's said in such a tone of quiet assurance that you often find yourself taking it as fact. What's that, Richard? The sun isn't going to rise tomorrow? Well, if Richard isn't panicking then I'm sure it's nothing to worry about.

When the troublemakers reached the lower floor, they'd begun to exchange blows in the half-hearted way that people do when they realize they can't stop without losing face. It wasn't particularly skilled combat, far from the choreographed, graceful to and fro we see in action movies. Actual fighting is rather ugly, clumsy and undignified, so they made it across the floor of the basement level without doing any more damage to each other than a boxed ear and wounded dignity. The party on the losing end of this struggle, clearly realizing that the encounter was not weighed in his favour, looked around for a weapon with which to even the odds.

He looked at the vast array of options, and there were many. He could have seized upon a selection of gigantic metal mortars stashed under the stairs by Georg. He could have picked up any of several large craft knives left hanging about the place by Stephen. Heavy books littered the room.

An ugly chair which was no longer fit for sitting on, but which would have made an excellent bludgeon. Truly, he was spoiled for choice. In fact, if he had chosen any of the above, it's highly unlikely anyone would have vouched to get in the way. Alas, the misguided soul chose to pick up a rolled-up poster from Richard's stack of carefully organized prints.

What exactly the Lesser Vagrant was hoping to achieve with this stratagem remains a mystery to this day, as his choice didn't really possess any characteristics of an effective weapon. He had barely seized the thin roll of paper, holding it aloft, when a shadow fell over him, and the two combatants realized possibly for the first time that they were not alone.

I think the idea of two strangers ruining his hard-won system roused some rarely seen but keenly felt sense of indignation in the phlegmatic depths of Richard's heart. A lesser man might have directly intervened and snatched the print from the hands of the enemy, even at the risk of damaging it, but Richard was no fool. Instead he drew himself up into a dreadful aspect, and in his usual manner informed them that the poster was very expensive, actually.

The two young men looked around. Something about Richard's dire countenance in that moment caused them to hesitate. After gently replacing the print with a muttered apology, I have never seen any two people leave the shop so fast, tripping up the stairs on the way out and falling through the doors in their desperation to get away as fast as possible.

I've tried to replicate this awe-inducing glare since, but I don't really have Richard's sense of gravitas.

38

A More Disastrous Kerfuffle

ONE EVENING JUST before closing, as the streetlights came on and an early sunset was descending on Sackville Street like the first clutches of Fimbulwinter, in came a man in an expensive-looking suit, wearing an entitled grimace. He was accompanied by a host of rumbling, tooting sound effects resonating from inside him that the shop acoustics only served to amplify. He radiated a sense that he was Bad News, and so the staff faded away from him as he wandered around knocking things over. As he trundled about the shop, he began to bellow. Not all customers are good enough to come over and ask for something in their inside voice – some of them like to boom. This man was a boomer. Soon, he began loudly to make requests that were not only obscene but which revealed him without any doubt to be that rare and unpleasant form of collector who specifically wants to indulge in atrocities by way of voyeurism. Perhaps it was a failure of mine, but in the moment I found myself frozen. I'd never thrown anyone out of the shop before, and I didn't know how to handle it.

If you work in rare books, it's only a matter of time before you stumble across something that shocks you. Golliwogs, Nazis and other reminders of humanity's failings are part of the book trade, as are the customers that for various reasons want to get their hands on them. Browsing the shelves of a rare bookshop, it's quite evident that we've spent most of our time on this floating rock doing awful things to each other. When you're handling sensitive material, you have to be prepared to handle a difficult topic very sensitively at a moment's notice. People often ring in asking for all kinds of uncomfortable books, and the right response can be elusive. I once had a man who rang in asking for, and I quote, 'a book about praying the gay away'. When he was tersely informed that this would not be possible, he switched tack to 'a book on how the Jews control the weather', at which I will admit to disconnecting him. It should probably concern us all that this is not the strangest nor the most offensive call that Sotheran's has ever received, but I digress.

When I arrived at Sotheran's, the prevailing attitude was that the golliwogs and suchlike should be placed in a cupboard where they were not on open display, a situation which seemed to keep everyone mostly happy. Initially, I thought that we didn't have much choice as a bookshop about who we sell our books to – the items follow the money for the most part. We do, however, go out of our way to try and sell sensitive material to institutions that will place it in the right context, and preserve it for the right reasons. There's never any question of whether a book is 'appropriate' – all books have something to teach us, but the nature of the lesson varies wildly. A copy of *Mein Kampf*, once owned by Marlene Dietrich, springs to mind. A vile book, and the world does not need more copies of it, but this one is made important by context.* It probably deserves to

---

* Dietrich was firmly anti-Nazi, and the copy was given to her while she was in Hollywood by Erich Maria Remarque, author of *All Quiet on the Western Front*, as a sign of all that was rotten in the Fatherland. Sotheran's has a

survive, in the right collection, which means we would need to market it with all the right context.

All this is worth keeping in mind, but I think one has to be guided by the cardinal rule which supersedes all others: one does not sell books to Nazis. A bookshop is not a court. As a custodian of books you can use your discretion to decide who you sell to, and unlike a court you don't have to give a reason. If you sell to one racist, you'll just attract more of them. It's your responsibility to try and make sure that important materials about topics like the Holocaust end up with institutions and with collectors who are not going to destroy them (and yes, this is absolutely a possibility). Some of you will undoubtedly baulk at this − 'it's not your job to decide whether I'll be a responsible owner', you might say. And indeed, we don't hand out a quiz to everyone who steps over the threshold, we assume people are fundamentally decent unless they show us otherwise. However, if it looks like a goose, honks like a goose and steps like a goose, then it's probably a Nazi, and there's honestly only one kind of person who complains when I say 'I don't sell books to racists', whatever they are calling themselves right now.

Blissfully, it's actually very difficult for anyone to tell if a bookseller doesn't want to sell them something. If we don't want to serve a monstrous person, they find themselves coming up against perfectly plausible hurdles, and there is

---

strictly No Nazis policy. Nazis don't get to have nice things like books or bookshops.

absolutely no way for someone to prove that those inconveniences are not genuine day-to-day bookshop accidents. A bad actor will find that whatever they want to buy, they end up hearing things like 'we lost the book' or 'it's on reserve, my mistake' or someone firmly telling them that 'there are no books on Africa' as they are guided away from a shelf marked Africa. In short, their behaviour is almost indistinguishable from a bookseller who *does* want to sell you something.

Which brings us back to our intruder.

As usual, it was James who came to the rescue, swooping in like the angel of death. I had never known James to turn down a sale for any reason until this day. There was no request which would faze him, none where he couldn't find at least one tangentially related book to sell, and yet on this day he had no intention of pandering. In a masterful and almost silent display, as if he were herding a single sheep, James had the man turned about and out of the door within minutes, and I'm not sure the chap even knew what happened.

I don't think James for a moment understood any of the nuances of discourse or had any aspiration to be a warrior for any kind of cause, but to me, it proved a point – everyone has to draw the line as to who they choose to sell to, and the choices that we make on those occasions will shape the kind of world we find ourselves in. The rare book trade might seem like it is located in its own sphere of existence, but it's not true. We are connected to the world by a thousand invisible strings, and each time we make sure a book on something unpleasant gets to the right place, or we block a homophobe from shopping with us, it's a tiny step in the right direction.

39

Bride and Groom

IT WAS TEN minutes before closing when she entered, clutching an array of carrier bags from expensive boutiques across the city. Face half shadowed under a gargantuan hat, she bustled through the doors with some difficulty before anyone could reach her, and then dumped her belongings on the floor. She had the air of someone at the very end of their tether, and so it was with extreme reluctance that I approached to offer my assistance.*

'I have to buy a gift,' she growled at me, throwing me a look which might have turned me to stone if I weren't avoiding eye contact. She kept staring, eyes wide open in some kind of furious fugue state, as this was apparently the extent of her contribution to the process. I stammered something about closing times, which she summarily ignored, taking off her furs and draping them over Dave the Owl's dusty bell jar.

In one of my rare proactive moments, motivated primarily by a desire to close up the shop and leave, I made the mistake of asking her what kind of books she wanted to look at. 'Well, he collects books,' she responded rather flatly. She looked around at the sea of books from across the ages, frowned, then clearly decided that she wasn't going to

---

* I had also noticed the Spindleman lurking outside, and I had no wish to be yet again fleeced for all our money by his wiles.

interrogate the vagueness of her own request as much as she was going to make it someone else's problem. 'I need to buy him a book,' she repeated. 'Something nice. You know?'

I did *not* know. This is something people do often in rare books – they march in very confidently looking for a tome, knowing someone who collects rare books, and only then do they realize that they haven't been listening. Purchasing a book for someone isn't like running to the shop and picking up a box of decorative soaps, or a bottle of whisky. You can't just take a stab in the dark and hope for the best. In the best-case scenario, a well-chosen book shows just how intimately you know a person, their interests, their politics . . . their very sense of self. In the worst case, it can show that you barely have any interest in who they are.

'My husband is a very serious collector,' she insisted, still looking around as if the answer might fall from the ceiling. 'He's very serious about his books. So I want to get him a nice book.' All I could do was nod, because the only rational thing to say, which was 'Why don't you know what kind of books he collects?', wasn't really an option if I wanted to get her out of the shop as quickly as possible. When people aren't sure what kind of book they are supposed to be buying, they ask for a 'nice' book or a 'good' book, possibly in the hope that the bookseller will look into a crystal ball and magically produce the right answer.

Fortunately, a book dealer trades in minor miracles. The trick is to lead the poor, beleaguered customer around the shop floor until you catch some kind of flash of recognition in their eyes. Recognition, and relief, because no one wants to turn up to their ever-suffering spouse on an anniversary with the wrong offering.

It's easy to think of book collectors, obsessive types and all, as solitary creatures who must surely live alone in their haunted castles, never to know the embrace of another living creature. However, the life of a book collector revolves around their families just as much, because invariably their chosen partner eventually finds their way to the bookshop with a thousand questions, plunging into the cold waters of the book world without a lifejacket. The things we do for love. The success they have is usually tied to the kind of collector they've hitched themselves to. Those who marry a Dracula have a hard task ahead of them, because they are limited to a very narrow sphere of potential gifts, and then they're likely to inadvertently buy something which doesn't fit the brief, or something the collector already has. The bigger the library of such a collector, the more desperate the family tends to be when it comes to the festive season and birthdays. Smaugs tend to be easier to please, because their collecting habits range further afield, and so a lucky family member can take a risk on something vaguely adjacent to their field of interest and hope for the best.

However troublesome this dynamic might seem on paper, it's far less worrisome than the alternative, in which the book collector chooses someone to share their life who considers their hobby to be an extravagance and a nuisance.

About once every three months we are blessed with the presence of a gentleman who looks a lot like a vole in a woolly jumper, if the vole had lived to seventy and had the dexterity of an Olympic gymnast. He wears a large hood, and always drags a small suitcase behind him, which rattles a bit because it's empty when he arrives. He furtively darts about the shop, looking for books on plants (which he enjoys), and takes his time selecting an array of items which will fit neatly into his suitcase. During the process of purchasing the books, he animatedly explains every time that he'll need to disguise the books in something so that they aren't obvious. I usually give him some newspaper or truss them up in something so that they can't be seen, though the parcels are still suspiciously book-shaped. Crowing, he packs them neatly into his case, telling us with a wicked grin that if his wife finds out then he is in a lot of trouble. He pays in cash, because he doesn't want there to be a paper trail, which I suppose speaks to exactly how involved this spousal game of cat and mouse has become.

The most sordid part of this story is that we get similar cases several times a week. The world of book collectors seems to be half full of those who are engaged in some form of protracted guerrilla warfare with their other half. Late into my apprenticeship, I even made a house visit to a chap with three floors of books (including a room which one couldn't access without jumping between clear patches of floor) who was only selling books to us because his wife had insisted that he remove some. We managed to buy about thirty before he clammed up and we never heard from him again, and by the pained look on his face when we made off with that first batch I predicted as much.

The problem, in a nutshell, is that collecting books is much more than a hobby. The sheer amount of space required to house most book collections means that whoever shares your living area needs to be very understanding, or more ideally a co-conspirator, because the rest of their lives will be spent making room for your incredibly invasive pastime, until one day they trip on a folio and plummet to their doom down a staircase.

The only real solution, I have begun to advise, is that your average book collector choose to live as a hermit. This is a foolproof way of avoiding judgement. Alas, in many ways the life of a book collector is doomed to the distraction of romance, if only because the zeitgeist is infected with the idea that a bookshop is a great place to romantically approach strangers, a plague for which romantic comedies have a great deal to answer.

As to the lady in the large hat, we found her a nice gift in the end, by the tried and tested method of throwing random books and authors in front of her until she saw a binding with enough gold on the side that it pleased her tastes. I supposed that if *he* didn't like it, then at least *she* would enjoy looking at it.

40

Correspondence

UNWANTED LETTERS ARRIVE at Sotheran's all the time – misplaced business mail (often addressed to staff members who haven't worked here in many years) and a steady stream of catalogues from other booksellers looking to entice us into spending money on yet more stock. As the apprentice, and the first barrier against the horrors of the outside world, there was a period when it was my responsibility to make sure these letters reached the right place. The local postmen, perhaps irritated by the fact that we receive more than our fair share of large, unwieldy parcels, have a habit of including in our mail any letter which they can't find any better use for. This would make for an extended diversion, with me ferrying letters first about the shop to people who absolutely did not want them and then into the street in a doomed attempt to unite them with their true owners.

Among the letters, there's usually a percentage which are handwritten, the reason being that it's hard to persuade some of our older customers that they can email us, and further to the point a good many of them don't even own a computer. Some are still struggling with the concept of the abacus. Regardless, the novelty of a handwritten letter never really fades, because it's impossible to say before you open it whether they want something really inconvenient from you or have a complaint to make. The best ones are sealed with wax, which I try to open first because I like to reward the kind of behaviour I want to see.

If we are very lucky, the letters in question will be that most cherished of communications, the handwritten thank you note. I have a little file containing all the thank you letters I have ever received, and I sometimes look at them if I'm having a particularly bad day. I don't know many other retail jobs where people write you heartfelt notes simply for doing what you're paid to do, but in rare bookselling it doesn't seem uncommon. I've had letters thanking me for sending books, when the courier charged an extortionate fee. I've had letters congratulating us on the release of a new catalogue, as if it were some personal literary endeavour and not an extended and rather heavy marketing ploy. I've had letters simply to talk about the weather, or from customers wishing to say hello while they were on holiday somewhere nice, and which had nothing at all to do with books.

Of all the nice letters I've ever received, the ones I hold particularly close to my heart were sent from a mysterious stranger masquerading as the bookshop-owning angel Aziraphale from the novel *Good Omens*, which were not only produced with meticulous attention to detail, but contained a number of angelic gifts into the bargain.* Now, we're not supposed to be biased, but the receipt of such a note almost always bumps the sender up in the queue from wherever they were before to a Person of Interest. Most of the staff have a little penpal of their own for whom they keep a candle burning, from the Effervescent Apiarist (a Dracula who is very grateful to be notified of any books even tangentially related to bees) to the Reclusive Abbess (who resides in Corfu but has her tiny letters sent from the mainland somewhere near the border of Albania because she is worried about them being intercepted).

I always told myself I would avoid getting drawn into

---

* My favourite remains a set of personalized bookplates, emblazoned with the motto 'estne volumen in toga an solum tibi libet me videre', which I believe translates roughly to 'Is that a book in your pocket, or are you just happy to see me?'

that kind of social entanglement, and I managed it for quite a few years until Chris received an inconvenient-looking letter from a man we shall call the Incarcerated Professor. (As the manager, anything directed simply to 'Sotheran's' often ends up with him first. It is one of the burdens of leadership.) It contained a list of academic books he wished to procure, on account of not currently being able to leave the house. He wished, in fact, to recon-struct his entire academic library from scratch, a process that would in theory be quite lucrative but promised to be about as interesting a task as ramming one's head repeat-edly into a wall. The letter sat on Chris's desk for a week or two before he made an executive decision and passed it to me. The letter then sat on my desk for a further six months before I received a tentative and very pleasant phone call from the man in question who was so reasonable about the simply outrageous delay that I spent the next week tracking down all the books in a fit of guilt. He then had the abso-lute audacity to send a thank you note, as if he were the one who had been utterly negligent, and this cycle has con-tinued ever since, with me performing a rather skeletal (and extremely tardy) version of my responsibilities and him thanking me far more than is really necessary given the circumstances.

Interestingly, since we've begun our slow and careful evolution into an online bookseller, we've been blessed with a glut of nice reviews from customers who I think would otherwise have held their opinions to their chest. Over the past few years a trickle of nice comments has become a flood of people remembering we exist, sharing memories of someone who helped them find just the right book through emails, reviews and social media. It's heartwarming to see those messages getting passed around.

On the other side of the coin, and more unpleasantly, come complaints. I keep a little file of the best of these too, which provides me with a perverse sort of merriment in dark moments.* The kind of complaints we get fall into two camps. The first are those that are completely factually correct but concern issues which we either don't consider issues or which are completely beyond our power to fix. Things like 'the shop was very quiet' fall into that category, because Yes Madam, You Are Describing A Bookshop; but we also get snippy letters in which people are upset that they didn't receive our latest catalogue in a timely manner, or that their parcel didn't arrive properly.† I have a time-honoured strategy for these which has yet to fail me: I mark them as 'important' or place them somewhere prominent on my desk where it's clear I intend to do something about them, and then I slowly let them grow stale for a few weeks, at which point I declare them void because it's long past the point where they would have expected a reply and I don't want to reopen a closed case.

---

* My favourite is a note which reads: 'Sotherans. I don't like it.'

† Increasingly, the modern customer expects us to maintain some kind of psychic control of a parcel once it leaves the shop. We are blamed for storms, criminally minded postmen, flat tyres, and a myriad of other logistical woes. I have become particularly adept at finding polite ways to say 'that's lovely, but ultimately we aren't to blame for the fact that your home address is at the bottom of an active volcano'.

41

The Snap

THERE'S A CUSTOMER trying to get my attention. He's been smiling loudly at me and creeping closer for about ten minutes, but he clearly wants me to address him first. Some kind of bizarre power play that I have no interest in entertaining. I'm six hundred pages into counting my way through a book, and one slip means I'll have to start again at the beginning, so I ignore him. He creeps about. Continues to stare. Eventually he pops up behind me with a cross-sounding 'I really need some help, you know, I have an important question'. I lose my place, and put the book down with a sigh.

He drags me over to the bookcase on the other side of the room, and spreads his hands wide for a moment as if trying to conceptualize it. I stand there. Looking and feeling annoyed. 'Can you . . .' he says, striking a thoughtful pose. 'Can you *explain* this bookshelf to me?'

The saying goes that once you've spent two years in the book trade, you remain there for life because you've become unemployable anywhere else. This anecdote has a ring of truth to it. Sotheran's has burned through many a promising youngster through the decades, the smartest of whom decided that the book trade was not for them,* but if

---

* I often think of Roisin, who lasted about a year and a half before moving to a remote village in Ireland without electricity or clean water to study pottery.

someone can finish two whole years of service, they are vanishingly unlikely to take up a job in another sector. It just doesn't seem to happen. However, I have been developing a more advanced theory that I think is more accurate: I believe that every bookseller eventually suffers something I call the Snap.

I'd been behaving myself for several years when the moment finally came for me. They don't tell you before you sign up to a bookshop that a significant part of your role has nothing to do with books, and everything to do with managing a host of colourful and fragile personalities. Oh, it's hinted at, to be sure, and I think an insightful person would read the room before taking the job. The rest of us, alas, go into it thinking that the brunt of our time will be spent on the books, which is proven horribly wrong at five minutes past six on a Friday evening when someone comes in to talk to you excitedly about their stamp collection, taking up several hours of your time as you pointedly sigh and make meaningful glances at the clock. During this time, the phone constantly rings with pointless queries. Cryptids surface to ask you sinister questions, flicking forked tongues. At the same time, you're expected to be cataloguing complicated books, counting hundreds of pages, and (crucially) not making mistakes at any point, or one of those phone calls will be from an outraged customer waving a receipt.

When you are first hired as a bookseller, you are inclined to try and make a good impression, practising all those reliable hallmarks of customer service you see on television. Everyone gets a hello and a half-hearted smile, no customer is in the wrong, yes *of course* I'll double-check for you, sir. And then, at a moment of pressure, comes the Snap.

To understand the context of the moment, we have to talk a bit more about Rebekah.

No one in this world has ever been a harder-working bookseller than Rebekah. She possesses that indefatigable spirit common, I think, to ancient heroes of legend. Watching her delve into the 'reserve cabinet', where we keep things we no longer want to think about, reminded me of Heracles mucking out the Augean stables. It wasn't so much that impossible tasks were placed on her plate so much as she *volunteered to take them on*, without so much as a word of complaint. If I finished everything urgent for the day, I would usually lope back to my desk and spend a few hours unwinding, perhaps tinkering with some riddle or mystery I'd been nursing. If Rebekah finished everything urgent, she would gut some long-forgotten cupboard and make sense of it, or she'd go through all the old book records and remove useless ones. She hit the ground running, and as I was used to something more akin to a waddle, eventually I had to ask her to slow down.* To this day I don't think she understood what I meant.

To summarize, Rebekah is like nothing I've ever seen in an antiquarian bookseller. Truly some kind of utterly fantastical worker bee, who we did not (and do not) deserve.

Which brings me to the Snap. It was a lazy bookshop

---

* It feels like one of those koans about trees falling in the forest. Am I a bad employee, or is Rebekah a good one? Perhaps both?

morning when the Imperious Gentleman walked in. He made a show of marching in as if he expected to be greeted with a fanfare or a carpet, and I instantly resolved to avoid him as best I could. He trotted about the shop, occasionally nudging a bookcase with his foot like a pig rooting for truffles, before his gaze homed in on Rebekah. She was busy on one of her thankless tasks which I did not want to interrupt, some grand enterprise which would make all of our lives easier, no doubt, and it looked complicated. He had that look in his eyes which men occasionally get when they see a woman working in a bookshop, that vaguely predatory aura which is easy to read as 'Ah, I've found someone who can't get away from my conversation and is obliged to be nice to me'. I am really not the kind of person who believes it's necessarily my place to interfere in situations where people can advocate for themselves, so I patiently sat back and tried to ignore him as he launched into a long and distracting monologue about his achievements directed at Rebekah, who did the professional thing and listened with a polite face while clearly itching to get back to her work. This was not the first time a man had made inappropriate advances on Rebekah through the shop, including asking to take her to lunch or trying to find ways to be alone with her in an enclosed space, and though obviously I respected her ability to deal with these situations in the way that she felt best, I am keenly aware of how vulnerable you feel in a new job, and how the instinct is not to make a fuss even if you feel uncomfortable.

An hour passed in this fashion, as he slowly began to get more and more offensive. He reached the point where he started to describe how women had brains smaller than men, which was why they were worse at exploring. Something snapped. I think it was at that moment when years of built-up resentment and frustration at completely unreasonable people with utterly nonsense demands broke my willingness to put up with it. It was at this exact point that I became completely unemployable anywhere else, because in that moment I lost the willingness to be polite to people who squander the benefit of the doubt. Reader, I did the unthinkable and interrupted him.

I will divert for a moment to talk about British custom and convention. One does not interrupt a customer. It's against British custom in the same way that you don't speak to people on a train, and how a crowd instinctively organizes itself into a queue. It's the kind of institutional politeness we use to avoid talking about or addressing bad behaviour. One does not correct a client openly, or speak one's mind to them. It's as close to punching them in the face as you can get without being thrown in jail. I had, in any way that counted, chosen violence.

Hell hath no fury, they say, like a man treated the same way as he treats women. He sputtered. He turned a shade of red that travelled upwards across his body as in a cartoon character, and to this day I would swear under oath that his head actually inflated a few inches.

I asked him to let us get on with our work, which caused him to spin into a spiral of angry comments, threatening to speak to the manager.* This was no way to do business, he

---

* Laughable.

raged. He'd just wanted to have a conversation, he bellowed. Did we treat all our customers like this? His impotent rantings continued until he ran out of steam, at which point I had already returned to what I was doing. Looking about as if he'd suffered some kind of traumatic experience, he made his way across the silent shop floor to the doors, which hit him in the back on the way out.

Rebekah snapped a few years later, when the same supplier called the shop with the same question for the fifth time in an afternoon. Georg snapped at birth, I think.

Decorative bust of John Milton, bearing characteristic grimace. Sold as a pair with more agreeable Shakespeare bust (not negotiable).

MODERN FIRST EDITIONS

A selection of modest cogitations regarding the advent of modern bookselling, the passing of time and other regrettable inevitabilities.

E NTERING THE TWENTY-FIRST century has been a challenge for the rare book trade. For one, people keep releasing new books, and though you can ignore them for a few decades, eventually you have to start paying attention. The department called Modern First Editions handles all the popular fiction, twentieth-century masterpieces, and anything else too current for comfort.

42

Into the Closet

I N THE QUEER COMMUNITY, there's a saying that you never really stop coming out of the closet. This is as true in a rare bookshop as it is anywhere else, though the extra cupboard space is often useful for storing books.

It's not that I didn't trust my new colleagues, you understand, but you don't last long as a gay book-loving nerd in this world without learning to conceal it from strangers until you're quite certain how they will react. Further, there are certain red flags one looks for when making that decision, and if a place is aesthetically stuck in the 1800s, then you can't help but wonder whether the people might be too. Mercifully, it's not the kind of issue that really comes up in a job interview, and I had the luxury of being able to wait until I felt comfortable.

It took me about a year to casually introduce it into conversation the way one does these days. If you're not familiar, it's very simple, you just suspiciously avoid gendered pronouns when discussing your other half for months and then one day drop one into the dialogue like a queer bouncing bomb and wait for the realization to hit.* Then you have to

---

* Now that I'm married, I simply have to contrive to mention the word 'husband', which makes the conversational hurdle substantially lower.

search the expressions of everyone around you for that tell-tale flinch of disappointment, and keep your back to the wall.

To my surprise, the bombshell (and I think the modern homosexual always believes somewhere in their soul that every single time they do it, it will end in disaster) hit the floor without a single sound. I was so surprised by the complete, almost offensive lack of reaction that I threw in a few more grenades just to make sure. If this seems like causing trouble to you, then you have to understand that I had worked in a number of theoretically progressive and forward-thinking workplaces, all of which had reacted with some level of irritating institutional bigotry ranging from 'So, who is the *woman* in your relationship?' to staring daggers into the back of my head for weeks. It simply didn't make any sense to me in the moment that a place as temporally stagnant as Sotheran's didn't care at all.

To my shock, and after repeated (ever more obvious) testing, it became clear that there was no drama to be harvested whatsoever. That being said, after a while I began to notice that James had started to introduce more queer authors and literature into the daily stock of books I was practising on. If I had somehow managed to miss the stacks of Oscar Wilde, or the little boxes of Isherwood, he also went to some lengths to draw my attention to them while pretending that the reason was something obscure to do with the binding, or the association. Never so many books as to provoke a conversation I may not have wanted to have, but enough for me to feel welcome. It was a kindness that I will not forget.

As I've grown in ability and confidence, I've become more able to see that my initial understanding of the situation was incorrect, and that I was very far from alone. All around me in the book trade there were people like me just going about their business, but more quietly than I do. I began to understand that in certain circles, and in book collectors of a certain age, they weren't going to come in and ask for gay literature. They weren't going to use any of the language I might use to describe myself, or that I'd find in modern queer books about our community. Instead, I've learned that many collectors of queer arcana will expect you to carefully watch what kinds of authors they ask after, and learn to take a hint when it is given. This doesn't stop me being openly delighted about it, but they'll have to take what they can get. This is a two-way street and they'll need to deal with the fact that I'm happy to see them.

Also, I take Gay Pride off as a holiday every year, something which I'm not prepared to compromise on, and which no one has yet been brave enough to argue with me about. Being open about who you are can be a little scary, but I think that after you've explored your first dungeon, or been hounded through a forest by an unknown threat, you begin to worry less about the approval of others and more about whether you remembered to bring a torch.

43

Health and Safety

YEARS AFTER THE Great Upheaval, when it had faded to an uneasy memory, we were still stumbling across the occasional hazard left by the workmen. After a while, dodging death on a daily basis became more aggravating than picking up the phone, so Chris put his managerial foot down and decided to get a professional in to check that the place was still fit for bookseller habitation. There are only so many dangling wires and ominously placed books at the top of stairwells one can pass by without feeling a tad uneasy, and I don't think he wanted to go to jail for losing a staff member to tetanus. 'Welcome, we're open' doesn't have a sincere ring to it if you know you're herding your customers into a tomb of horrors.

Plans were made. Quiet phone calls were conducted. One bright Tuesday afternoon, as the sun began to warp the prints in the window, a confident health and safety inspector turned up at our door, looking for all the world like he'd stepped out of the first tranquil scene of a horror movie. He was the very picture of a man who mistakenly believed he had already experienced the worst the world could throw at him. (I should tell you that if Sotheran's had ever received a health and safety visit before this poor lamb stepped over the threshold, there was no evidence of it.)* A

---

* A curling and very faded poster, half occluded by boxes, exists somewhere in the reaches of the basement. It reads DON'T in big letters before being cut off, and it's no longer clear what it is forbidding us to do.

brief shadow of doubt passed over the inspector's expression as he stepped inside, as if some animal instinct were screaming at him to run while he still could.

Wielding his briefcase like a shield, he stopped for a moment to take in his surroundings. Welcomed inside, he stepped over an array of boxes placed thoughtfully near the top of the stairs, and introduced himself to Chris. A conversation followed in which the inspector explained he was just there to take a look around and fill out a brief questionnaire about daily life at the shop.

As he walked about, he began to ask tentative questions about things he was seeing but couldn't comprehend, like a man trapped in an Escher painting. Those ladders, he said, pointing at the offending articles, were interesting decorative pieces. The ladders in question were brought over from a previous iteration of the shop, and are older than the building. They have exactly one dimension, and are usually propped up against a shelf so a bookseller can scurry up them quickly, before they collapse. Speed and agility are the determining factors, and the best way to reach the top is to give it something of a running start. One learns to listen for creaking to determine precisely when they are about to fail. I personally learned to stop using them after I almost crashed through a glass case to my death, shielded only by the fact that the glass for the case in question was forged in the fires of Mount Doom and was therefore indestructible. It was explained to the inspector that we really did need the ladders, as without them it was impossible to reach the highest shelves, from which teetering books would capriciously fling themselves, plummeting to the shop floor at near-lethal velocity.*

Moving on, he was slowly and ever more reluctantly walked through more of the shop's inbuilt safety hazards. Yes, that nail has always been there. No, we're not sure where that hatch goes, but if something hasn't emerged after all these years then it probably isn't going to any time soon. After examining the stairwell lighting, only fixable by mounting a wooden plank over the edge and walking slowly across the creaking boards above the chasm, the inspector changed his tack. Fire safety! He latched on to it as if it were a lifeboat. Surely a bookshop like this one, a veritable tinderbox of flammable and precious items, would have a robust fire safety procedure?

We finally located the water fire extinguisher hidden behind a spiral display of books near the stairwell and for certain out of reach without both destroying the display and risking a tumble head over heels into the dark. It was a victorious moment. Expectations had incrementally lowered with each passing minute, and when it was presented to him he seemed almost relieved. It needed replacing, naturally. We were also supposed to have two kinds, in case of

---

* I recall in particular a gigantic, rather lavish photobook called *Aphrodisias* up on the top shelves. *Aphrodisias* is the work of Turkish photographer Ahmet Ertuğ, who was for a period very fashionable if you wanted to dominate your sitting room with a huge book of tasteful antiquities. One late afternoon, some quirk of fate caused the humongous tome to fall forward, breaking out of its wooden prison and crashing to earth like a comet. It missed someone by less than a foot. On inspection, *Aphrodisias* was unharmed, though I cannot say the same for the floorboards.

electrical fires, but clearly whoever had been in charge of procuring this one had deemed it to be sufficient. The amount of dust it was trailing arguably made it a hazard itself, and it wheezed a bit when he tried to get a closer look.

The further he went into the shop, the more desperate he seemed to get. He turned away from one hazard only to be confronted by the sole fire exit, which had been turned into more of a fire obstacle course by boxes. On being informed of the Other Cellars (which must be perfectly safe, or how could someone be living down there?) he turned a peculiar shade of grey, and needed a sit down. A chair was provided, but he couldn't sit on it for long because it was really more of a decorative seat – sitting on it threatened to plunge the user through the middle and back on to the floor.* At this moment, Georg wandered by holding a dinner tray made of a thousand tiny butterfly carcasses, prompting the poor man to escape into the packing cellars. The cellars full of buckets and water leaking on to the electrics.

I think, to a man who spent most of his day using a checklist to make sure that people were lifting boxes in the right way,† this was like living through one of those horror

---

* This was one of many chairs that once populated the upper floor, none of which were fit for service. We threw away almost all of them during the Upheaval, but kept one out of sentimentality. There's a knack to noticing someone is about to sit in it, and rushing over to warn them before they get stuck in a very undignified position.

† We were not.

movies where the protagonists are killed one by one in a series of deadly traps. Then, there in the cellar, the boxes rustled a bit in the inexplicable way they do sometimes (which I attribute to an unseen cryptid) and the inspector fled out into the daylight. He did not return.

We've placed a new health and safety poster downstairs in the basement, in honour of his valiant attempt, but I don't think anyone has really noticed. And we did get a new fire extinguisher, in the end, and put it somewhere where we might reach it in a crisis. The thought of all those books going up in smoke was too anxiety-inducing not to. As we looked for a place to put it, I saw the shop clearly again for the first time in a long while, and I couldn't help but wonder when it was that I'd stopped internally criticizing the leaky roof, the dodgy clock, the boxes piled up in odd places. There had come a point where those things had faded into the background, where their absence would irritate me more than their presence.

44

The Spindleman Returns

THE SPINDLEMAN HAS returned, and he has me in a bind. He's brought some books in that I actually want this time, and he is snickering to himself about it in a corner. He's rustling something under his coat and (I presume) cleaning his hidden mandibles. He has already laid down his gauntlet, asking me what I am prepared to pay him for them. It's a sneaky move, because it places the responsibility on me to get the prices right, or risk proving myself incompetent (and a mark for future skulduggery). He's testing me. I make a move towards my computer, and his eyes flicker in distaste. Will I need the crutch, he's quietly assessing.

The internet is a polarizing topic of conversation for anyone in the book trade. Depending on who you ask, it either ruined everything or it saved everything. Truthfully, this is one of those situations where the answer is probably somewhere in the middle. Of everyone, it seems most frequently to be customers who have a grievance with us using the internet for work, even if it's something a bookshop has to master in order to compete in the modern world. I think people would prefer to believe that we still do everything in books, and with quills, but in actuality booksellers have developed something of a hybrid method of working. One could perhaps fill an entire book by itself with theories about why it has taken certain parts of the rare book trade so long to embrace the internet, but regardless of the why, Sotheran's was late to the game.

I think the real coup, what really pushed the book dealers over the edge into accepting it, was the way the instant communication was changing the book market. The ability in no time at all to compare the prices of books against your competitors almost caused the book trade to shatter into pieces, and that's because there's still no hard and fast rule about how to price a book. You have to try and sell it for more than you paid for it – it's the only way to keep the lights on – and yet if your prices are too high you'll lose custom. If you underprice a book, then it will sell immediately (usually to another dealer, who will swoop in twirling their moustache to make a tidy profit); if you overprice it, you could be stuck with it as the seasons turn into years, and the years turn into decades. And so, faced with every price from £1 to infinity, you base your evaluation on similar things you've seen over the years, and hope it sells (but not too quickly).

It's not unusual for collectors and dealers to ask for discounts on the price when they make a purchase. In fact, it's common enough that many established collectors make it their first question. We're English, though, so the discussion is often couched in euphemism. You'll frequently hear people asking for the 'best price' on a book, which is a roundabout way of saying 'this is daylight robbery, and you belong in jail, but I will settle for a generous discount'. As an apprentice bookseller, you have to be able to navigate these constant requests with as much grace as possible – you don't want to offend anyone, but you do also want to make some money. The wheeling and dealing around the fair price is central to the experience of being a book dealer, and being in a coalition of booksellers like Sotheran's only adds to the underlying tension. One often finds oneself in the position of having to sell books from a colleague's department, and the temptation to offer whatever incentive is necessary to sell the book is tempered by the fact that you'll have to explain to that same colleague the next day why you thought you could slash a third of the price from the most expensive book on their shelves. (Alternatively, you can just hide from them until everyone forgets, which is my preferred survival method, but each to their own.)

People get very into their haggling, and for some people the haggling is even part of the fun. Unlike most other shops, where no one would ever consider debating with the cashier over the price of, say, a piece of meat, people feel uniquely entitled to argue over the price of a book. It's something of a performance in and of itself, where you act as if the customer is dragging you over hot coals, and they act as if you're trying to sell them snake oil. We have many familiar customers who go through the entire routine every time, even if they know that we're going to give them the same discount we always do. I genuinely believe that the pantomime is important to them, and none of the staff seem to mind as it gives us a chance to practise giving people bleak looks and haunted smiles. This charade gets rather intricate when it involves customers who play a five-year-long game of returning annually to look at a book, making pointed remarks about how they 'saw it here last year'.

I push the books back across the counter to the Spindleman. I'm borrowing a trick from James, confided to me late one lazy Saturday afternoon. I'm just so swamped, I say, gesturing around me to all the books on my desk (the Spindleman doesn't need to know that these tasks are not necessarily urgent). Truly *swamped*. If the Spindleman wants to do business, he'll have to suggest some prices, throw some ballpark figures out there, or how will I ever find the time to help him? He understands, surely? Like Rumpelstiltskin being told his own name, the Spindleman stamps his feet so hard he almost descends through the floor right back to hell. Casting me a dark look, he pulls out a list of suggestions he has already prepared, and clearly hoped he would not be forced to provide.

Today, the victory is mine, and it is an odd feeling. I've been sparring with the Spindleman for years, on and off. Finally to get the better of him feels like the culmination of a life arc, though there's no one here with whom to share the victory. All the other booksellers are out, and I realize that I've been trusted to look after the bookshop alone. An odd feeling. The next day, I am given a key to the shop, so I can come and go as I please.

45

Working for Exposure

I SAW SOME GOURDS on your website,' a man with a handle-bar moustache told me, leaning over the counter with a raised eyebrow. He was holding a large umbrella like a spear, as if at any moment he might turn round and use it to stick a charging boar.

I blinked. 'Gourds?'

'Yes,' he confirmed, with an impatient wave of the hand. 'Gourds. Carved with the face of Queen Victoria. I'd like to see them.'

I looked around in amazement to see if anyone else was hearing this. They were not. My mind turned involuntarily to the smashed gourds hidden somewhere in a cupboard. Until now, my sole defence against the guilt of their destruction had been my confident daily mantra that no one would ever have purchased such a ghastly item anyway, an illusion which was being rudely dispelled before my very eyes.

I pretended to have a good look around for the broken gourds, actively opening cupboards and rustling in a busy way, while avoiding the dark box where I knew I had buried the bodies. After wasting as little of his time as I could without admitting that my entire performance was a calculated charade, I diverted him to a bookshelf instead where he forgot about fruit-related enquiries entirely.

This, friends, is the real danger of a more connected world. You see, after I murdered the gourds, I made a fatal error in forgetting to erase them from the electronic system. When I'd first arrived at the shop, this would never have come to light, because the website was more of an afterthought and you couldn't find anything if you wanted to. My secret would have gone with me to the grave. The passage of years, however, and the increased reliance on that most double-edged of swords, social media, proved my undoing.

Social media is one of those skills that everyone thinks they'd like to be good at, until they realize that it actually just involves managing thousands of emotional strangers for twenty-four hours a day, seven days a week. In my hubris, and worried that I wasn't able to pull my weight alongside people with two decades more experience, I thought to make myself useful in taking over one of the social media accounts. It had, until that point, retained a quiet dignity which didn't do anyone any harm, but the folly of youth overcame me.

The unfortunate part of this story is that I really am good at it. Most antiquarian booksellers retain a healthy suspicion and derision for the entire concept of social media, reluctantly posting a picture of a book once every month or so as if paying tribute to a hostile village spirit. The resentment at being forced to resort to this ... this *barbarism* is etched without any humour at all into their every word. You can almost hear some of them sulking through the screen.*

To my mind, the solution was (and remains) simple. Social media is like a cat: it can tell if you're only pretending to like it, and it will claw you. If you're afraid of it, because you're afraid of seeming like you don't know what you're doing, then you're missing the point, which is that the entire platform is thousands of people all desperate to acknowledge that they have no idea what they are doing, revelling in the fact that expertise is just the end result of a long series of mistakes. Sure, there are oddballs and bad characters to contend with in the same way as in real life, but it's possible to form meaningful bonds using the strange combination of honest mistakes, wry humour and sincere enthusiasm that are familiar to anyone who spends their working life in a bookshop.

This approach has not always gone down well with

---

* The antics of booksellers who have no idea what they are doing on the internet will always bring me joy. One of our competitors once got cross with us and left us a two-star review on Google, under his own name, presumably thinking it was anonymous. It's still up there.

some of my colleagues in the trade. I have cultivated at least one nemesis who routinely complains about my antics to the Booksellers Association, who rather distractedly notify us both every time that schoolyard spats don't really come under their purview. In many ways, this bookseller is one of my oldest and dearest correspondents, though I suspect he shall never know it.*

That being said, the general response has been slightly overwhelming. With increased exposure to the world comes increased traffic through our website, which results in people finding records and buying items that we can't find. Lately, a day rarely goes by when we don't get an alert warning us that some treacherous internet delver has attempted to buy an item we last saw five years ago. Old customers who had forgotten we existed have been re-emerging from the mycelium, and we have been submerged in people trying to sell us things we don't want.

Opinion is still divided over whether this new influx of chaos is causing more busy work than actual sales, but Pandora's box has already been opened and there's nothing to do but hope for the best. I am of the experimental opinion that in the strange world we now occupy, rare bookselling is a numbers game. James would always tell me that you could have the strangest book in the world, and that if you kept it long enough someone would want it – there's someone for every book. The logical extension of that attitude to me is

---

* If you're out there, and reading this, then I want you to know that you have no sense of humour and your complaint letters are the nectar of life to me.

that if that's the case then you want to show all those books to as many people as possible. For instance, we had a book on paintings that had been in the shop since before Andrew even joined the company. Decades. Long enough that we stopped having records for when exactly it was bought. That book was posted on social media and bought within an hour.

It's unclear what this means for the world of rare bookselling in the long run, but it gives me hope that in a world of rising costs and unreliable tides, we might be able to reach a new audience that allows us to keep doing the curmudgeonly work we do best. Maybe it would be best if they don't turn up all at once, though. I only have so many broken gourds to sell.

46

No-Sniff Zone

SHE SWEPT IN with the air of a grand duchess about to announce that she'd located the lost princess Anastasia. Behind her, she trailed a boy with the same resigned look on his face that I recognized from being dragged around clothes shops in my youth. She stopped to breathe in the atmosphere, evidently enjoying every moment of the experience, and then checked to make sure that her charge was doing the same. He was not, because he'd spied a seat in the corner of the room (there was no way he could have known the seat was a deathtrap) and was edging slowly towards it. Chivvying him further inside, she managed to lock eyes with me against my will, marching in my direction as I tried unsuccessfully to look like I was very occupied.

Peering over the pile of books I'd slid in the way as a barricade, she fixed me with the wry look people give me when they *know* they are about to make an unreasonable request. 'I'm not here to buy anything,' she said, and I had to appreciate her honesty as she prepared to waste precious time I was perfectly capable of wasting by myself, 'but I have a question that you might think is a bit strange.' She gave me another knowing look, and I began to think, as I sometimes do, how my funeral would look if this stranger pulled a knife out on the shop floor and gutted me like a fish.

I gave her a weak smile, which she correctly interpreted as a sign she should continue. 'I'm taking my grandson,' she said, 'on a smell tour of London.' We had to stop there while she explained to me what a smell tour was. The way she characterized it, a smell tour relies on the fact that the brain interprets and stores scent memories in a different, longer-term way to sight or sound, and she'd been taking her grandson to lots of different places in London with intense 'smell profiles' so that if he ever encountered those smells again as a grown man, it would bring back memories of her after she was gone. This sentiment thawed my icy indifference just a little, so when she asked for an old book to smell, I begrudgingly fetched something suitable.*

---

* It seemed like they had come for the whole experience, so I found a dusty Latin copy of *The Iliad*, bound in heavy leather. I am not above a little showmanship when the occasion calls for it.

Something we've encountered far more often as we've been opening our doors to the twenty-first century is the kind of footfall that doesn't really translate into money, spurred by an underlying philosophy of books as objects to be fetishized for their smell, sound and feel. Not a day goes by but someone comes in and confesses that they're really just here because they love the smell, or because they felt the need to be around books. Some ask us to open cupboards because they want to touch something. There's something quintessentially human about the need to be around books, and in taking comfort in their presence. Book tours are far more frequent than they used to be, with large groups wandering from shop to shop, treating them more as sightseeing destinations than anything else. This irritates the people trying to get on with serious work, but when I see them cross the threshold into the silence and their faces take on that same awe that I felt the very first time I entered Sotheran's, my heart softens a little, and I understand.

47

The Price of Everything

I WANT YOU TO identify this book for me,' said an overbearing lady, shoving into my face her phone with which she had taken a blurrily unhelpful photo of a book. At least, it might have been a book. Like most people, including myself, she was not blessed at birth with that innate sense of light and perspective which results in a good photographer, and so her picture was less useful than if she'd done a chalk drawing of it on the pavement. In response to this query, I did what I always do and asked her if she would send over any pictures she had, and I would see what I could do. The moment I suggested email, her face settled into an expression of veiled distaste with a speed clearly born of practice. 'I don't want to send an email,' she said, waving her smartphone at me. 'I don't want to use a website. I want to speak to a real person.' The real person in front of her, to whom she was speaking quite rudely, explained (in as polite a tone as I could manage) that to answer her question would require her to give us the pictures, and unless she planned on spitting out ink like a squid and printing it herself then she'd have to do it electronically. The door closed behind her halfway through my explanation, as she yelled something about visiting one of our competitors.*

Booksellers have a bad habit of allowing themselves to be characterized as whatever people need from them in the moment. If someone needs you to clean up their vomit, then you're a retail worker. That same person will come in the next day demanding the help of someone who knows Latin, and suddenly you're a specialist. Flip flop. Back and forth. There's a dissonance between how a certain kind of person treats retail workers, and how they treat people they

---

* Not the most effective threat. She'd likely have got better results if she'd refused to leave and made herself my problem.

perceive as experts, and in a bookshop people tend to flicker confusingly between the two as if they aren't really sure whether they should keep being rude to you, or if you should start being rude to them instead.

In my opinion it's the access that does it. Resourceful experts wall themselves into the cellar of a university, or up in the highest room of a wizard tower, correctly assuming that contact with strangers can only ever lead to trouble. A rare bookshop is one of those liminal places where the public feel they have instant access to a specialist without having to, for instance, make an appointment. Or pay a fee.

Requests for valuations take up a vast amount of our time in the bookshop, and frankly they've only become more outrageous as more people have discovered we exist. The communal inbox fills up with emails that used to start 'Dear Sotheran's, I hope I could steal a moment of your time' but now are just blank with 'VALUE??' written in the subject line and a bunch of shady pictures attached. My willingness to engage with anything in the communal staff inbox has decreased over the years, taking a sharp dive once I realized that I was actually doing more harm than good by trying to politely inform people that their books weren't of interest to us – the judgement was always seen as some kind of open-ended debate, doomed to upset them and have me typing out fruitlessly apologetic emails late into the evening.*

---

* 'Nothing? My grandmother collected this set of fruitbat-adjacent novellas for decades! I demand a second opinion' etc.

Unfortunately for anyone who comes in insisting we value something for them, it's not actually a service most bookshops even provide. When buying, you figure out in your head how much you think you can practically charge your best customer for it, and then offer the person you're buying it from a healthy fraction of that. At no point in that process do you look at an item and say 'Well, I know exactly how much that item is worth' because it's never guaranteed that even your most reliable customer will actually buy it in the end. Your best assessment of the price of a book one night can be completely superseded by the events of the next day, if another copy turns up in a shop down the road (which has been known to happen).

So, when someone asks you to value their book, you might think it would be simpler just to do your best, give them a number you think is sensible and fair, and guide them firmly out of the shop. What harm could it do? They'd be happy, and I'd have peace and quiet. This would be true, if it wasn't for a rather regrettable trend that periodically emerges in the book trade, which is the advertising of books as investments. You can see how a bookseller makes the jump – it's an easy sell. Books are *almost* like art, so they must hold value in the same way. Some collectors like to think of their books as investments. Objects which will act, effectively, as a store for money until they're ready to sell the book and 'withdraw the funds'. Some of those even expect the book to grow steadily in value over time. To me it seems almost criminally optimistic of any rare bookseller to sell a book on those terms. Alas, there have been too many cases of outraged customers finding that they've lost everything because their beloved writer fell out of fashion, or because a style of leather binding is no longer the prevailing taste, so it's a practice that's generally frowned upon (though you'll still find some booksellers doing it if they think they can get away with it).

Where people get confused is that all booksellers need to buy books, and to do that they'll make an offer of money for them. It isn't the same as a valuation, because it's inherently a risk on the part of the bookseller. They don't actually know if they can make the money back on the book until they try. Given that some books have been on the Sotheran's shelves for over thirty years without (yet) selling, I think it's brave to assume that a single bookseller's opinion is secure enough ground on which to value your entire estate (and yes, we get frequent requests for us to go and sign off on that kind of thing, as if we can wave a pen and say that your castle of early Italian novellas is going to stand the test of time in the same way as gold).

It's strange to think that an industry built on so fragile and volatile a thing as the rare book could last a decade, let alone centuries. It almost feels like an intricate house of cards, with each of us holding a single piece in place, afraid to take our eyes off it in case the whole thing comes tumbling down. A wonderful, collective dream not guided by any conventional rule of economics but kept alive entirely by the fact we all *want* to believe – we *know* that the book we hold in our hands has value, it's in our bones, and if we will it hard enough then someone else will believe it too.

48

Bargain Bucket Bonanza

I'M STUCK UNDER a table. Maybe it's the sedentary lifestyle and the fact that there are five sandwich shops within a minute's walk from here, but I'm almost certain I used to fit under here without a problem. While trapped, I take the time to have a rifle through some of the boxes. I uncover four table legs, with no table in sight. A sock that might fit a baby, that's been chewed on by something. A toolbox containing only a damp rag, and a crowbar marked 'for domestic use'. By the time I am finally rescued, I have located a box full of blue poetry books. The books are Victorian, cheaply produced, and James chances by to ask me to put the pirated Tennyson back where I found it. It won't be considered scarce if anyone knew we had all the remaining copies, he reminds me.

With modern times comes a need to take stock of one's surroundings, and over the years we began to realize that we'd accumulated quite an array of stock that no one really knew how to sell. Whole departments of books gathered by people who were no longer with us, all gathering dust and taking up space that was making it hard to squeeze more books on to the shelves. Some gentle hints drifted down from the Powers that perhaps it would be a good idea to try and sell in bulk any books we didn't need. I think they were under the misapprehension that we'd be able to quickly sell the books and recover their cost price.

We began the process of jettisoning dead weight. The first bright idea was to pass on sets of books to burgeoning booksellers just starting out, and so a cache of valuable books on art were packaged up and sent overseas to someone we never heard from again. Every year the Accounts department ask us if we know what happened to that collection, and I tell them that the guy probably ran off with them and that we'll never see him again. I think they mark him down as 'pending' or something.

Next came the idea of a spring sale, but as there was no advertising of this beyond a few petulantly crafted signs tucked into the cases where no one could see them, it was not a resounding success. In fact, James looked so furious whenever anyone so much as mentioned the sale that the entire event went largely unpromoted.* The sale lasted for three months, and I think the only thing that sold was a coincidence when someone stumbled across the case and dared to take a peek inside despite the fact it was blockaded by boxes.

These avenues having failed us, and time moving ever onwards, we started to lean on other contacts to shift books. The more of them we pulled from the walls, the more we discovered, and I found myself sitting on gigantic stacks of suspiciously modern and incredibly dense books about arguably quite niche subjects, from stained glass to country houses. Ordinarily, I suppose Sotheran's would have waited a decade or two until they were rarer, but the Powers interceded on behalf of reason and so the books were packaged off to auction. Rebekah was delighted at the opportunity to

---

* James, that splendid and most determined recycler of staplers and paper scraps, found the entire notion of a clearout completely reprehensible.

make a list, and quickly got out her notepad to start arranging it. Georg came by to take some books for himself (though he insists he is not collecting them, per se). I have to assume to this day that we have some blackmail material on our contact at the auction house, because they kept accepting lots until they fell into insolvency, at which point we switched to a different auction house which should have known better than to keep taking our calls. They did, in fact, stop taking our calls after a while, but we kept sending them books anyway and as the boxes never returned it has been chalked up as a win.

People react very strangely to the idea that you might ever throw out a book, and as a rare bookseller you have to walk a strange line. On the one hand, your entire trade is based on the fact that some books are more important than others, and you have to make calls every single day about which ones to put a price label on and which ones to ignore. On the other hand you have people out there organizing smell tours of London who, if you act like you might need to do the sensible thing and recycle a book which you couldn't pay someone to take away, treat you like you've confessed to a long career of vandalism. They do not, at any point in their diatribe, offer to take the book off your hands.

This, I think, is the fate of the rare bookseller. You buy books, you sell them, and then you look after the ones which don't have anywhere else to go. Maiden, mother, crone. As the years pass, some books become familiar faces, even old friends which you pass by in the annual stock take. You'll touch a copy of *The Golden Ass* which you bought thinking it would sell immediately (you were wrong), and behind it you'll see a book about rats which you purchased in a moment of weakness from the Spindleman, and that you knew you had no chance of selling from the very beginning. Alongside them, each of the books you can see was bought by a bookseller who had a good (or bad) reason for it at the time.

Passing along the shelves, it feels like a strange calendar of days, a reminder of mansions and dungeons, cellars and railway platforms. I start to open a glass case with my keys to take a look at a book I don't remember buying, but James is there by my side in an instant, chiding me about my rough approach. It takes a 'soft, soft touch' he says. I could open it myself, but it's been a while since I asked his advice, and I know he still sees me as the lost boy who stepped over the threshold all those years ago. He wants to help, so I let him do it for me. Alas, there's little time to reminisce as a loud, angry knocking on the shop window suggests someone has failed to read the opening hours sign right in front of them. Reminiscing will have to wait until tomorrow.

Endings

I WAS CLEARING A display at the back of the shop when I uncovered a desk which I hadn't noticed before. I'd mistaken it for a table, in truth, because that's how it was being used. Once I'd moved off the mounds of photobooks, I was able to open the drawers and take a peek inside. Mounds of files. Reference books. Stationery. A tape measure and a magnifying glass. The tools of the trade, all gathering dust in a forgotten workstation buried under piles of books. I finished setting up the new display, but later on I made sure to casually ask Evelyn about the abandoned desk. It turned out it had belonged to a bookseller who'd died from a sudden illness some years before I'd arrived. The desk had never been cleared, and had slowly been assimilated into the furnishings.

Several weeks later, I found myself in need of a book stand, and took the tablecloth off another display to reveal yet another archived desk. This one carried the papers of a former director, which remained exactly as he'd left them when he departed. I put those back too. It seemed somehow disrespectful to tamper with them, even if we could have used the space.

These bookselling legacies aren't shrines in the way anyone would usually understand the word. They're just objects, left there because no one wanted to move them, and in time I suppose there will be no one left who remembers why they were important. Eventually, a new bookseller in need of a measuring tape will open one of those drawers and find exactly what they were looking for, a gift from the past.

James died a few years ago now, but you can still find him in the shop if you look closely enough. The stool he repaired over and over, the one he liked to sit on, is used to store travel books downstairs. His scrawled notes still appear in some of the books. The curved case he would use as a writing desk when his own was too messy is used to hold miniature books. His mug is in the kitchen. A box of confused and completely disordered old papers marked 'James Filing' lives in a cupboard. We don't need the papers any more, but I put them back each time exactly where I found them.

I cleared out most of my desk on the day I wrote this. Moving out of the city to spend some more time at home, with my husband. There are strange and wonderful books to be found out in the wild, and I intend to see them. I'll be coming down to the shop once in a while, to drop off some books and check the ceiling lights haven't fallen in, but it feels a lot like a goodbye. My new desk, given to me just as I no longer need it and finally big enough for me, I'll have to leave behind.

There's a new bookselling apprentice arriving on Monday, which I suppose means I am not the apprentice any more. I'm not sure exactly when that happened, but it must have done. I put some bookselling tools in the top drawer where they'll find them. I remove some books I want to take with me and leave behind some I think they might find useful. When they open the drawers, they'll find a scattering of old letters (including a glowing review from an ancient mariner), a tin of tuna, a selection of old keys (unmarked), a single water-damaged old boot and two broken, hideous gourds.

BOOKSHOP – THE GAME

A miniature bookselling RPG by Oliver Darkshire.

You are a bookseller.

Rent on your shop is due in 10 days.

You'd best start selling some books.

RULES

You have three scores: *Money, Time & Patience*

MONEY starts at 0

TIME starts at 10

PATIENCE starts at 10

A NEW DAY AT THE SHOP

To start your day, generate a new Bookshop Event by rolling a six-sided die. Adjust your scores as directed by the event, then roll a new event.

Keep rolling new events until your Patience or Time reaches 0. If your Patience reaches 0, you shut the bookshop early in a bad mood. If your Time reaches 0, it's closing time.

(At the start of each new day, reset your Time and Patience to 10. If your Patience reached 0 the day before, your maximum Patience is reduced by 1 . . . permanently.)

After 10 days, the Landlord arrives to collect 10 Money from you. If you don't have enough, the bookshop folds and you go out of business!

TABLES

A new Event . . .
(roll a die)

1 or 2 • a customer (see table below)

3 or 4 • a crisis (see table below)

5 or 6 • a peculiarity (see table below)

A customer!
(roll the die)

1 • Wants the bathroom .... −1 Patience

2 • Shoplifter .... −1 Money

3 • Wants a book you don't currently have...... −1 Time

4 • A literal wild animal .... −1 Time

5 • Has a complaint .... −1 Patience

6 • Buys a book .... +1 Money

A crisis!
(roll the die)

1 · You run out of tea .... −1 Patience

2 · The printer breaks .... −2 Time

3 · You can't find a book .... −3 Time

4 · Someone is haggling .... −3 Patience +1 Money

5 · The phone rings .... −2 Time

6 · You bought more books .... −2 Money

A peculiarity!
(roll the die)

1 · Mysterious noises to investigate .... +2 Time

2 · A feeling of dread .... −1 Patience

3 · A long, blissful silence .... +1 Patience

4 · Books fall off a shelf .... −1 Money

5 · You find a missing book .... +1 Money

6 · Unexpected bills .... −3 Money

OPTIONAL RULES

− spend 2 Money to refill your Patience to 10 by whatever vice takes your fancy

− for extra realism, you can play a 30-day month, but the landlord will expect 30 Money at the end of it . . .

Acknowledgments

THIS BOOK OWES ITS EXISTENCE almost entirely to the inspired hallucinations of John Ash at PEW Literary, my agent, who contacted Sotheran's out of the blue, and whom I rewarded by accusing him of being a fraud. I have never been more pleased to be wrong. There's also space, I think, to thank Alex Christofi at Transworld for seeing something in my ramblings, and then somehow turning those into a book. I barely helped either of them; in fact I'd go so far as to say I was an active hindrance to their efforts.

A special thanks is required, I think, to Chris Saunders, the managing director at Sotheran's, for entertaining the notion of this book and not throwing me out of the room for suggesting it. His continued support, and his notes, have been more valuable to me than I think he realizes. I owe a debt to all of my colleagues at Sotheran's for tolerating my antics all these years, and I hope they look on this project with indulgence.